YOU'RE PRETTY BUT DUMB

Ridiculous True Stories From One Woman's Hilarious Life

KIMBERLY VUZ

HOUSE OF INDIGO

COPYRIGHT

Created with Vellum

CONTENTS

Acknowledgments vii
Introduction xi

RIDICULOUS MISUNDERSTANDINGS

1. You're Pretty But Dumb 3
2. You're Going to Kill It 6
3. What Did You Just Say? 9
4. Wake Up, Or I'll Shoot 12
5. So, You're Presbyterian? 15

HOW EMBARRASSING

6. 'The Ass Man' 19
7. Too Much Junk 22
8. Ma'am, Can You Pull Up Further? 25
9. The Sex Show 28
10. Jersey Girls Don't Pump Gas 31
11. Confusion And Disgust 34
12. A Trail of Destruction 36

HOLIDAYS AND MISHAPS

13. Merry Effin' Christmas 41
14. More Shrimp Dip, Anyone? 44
15. Turkey Wars 50
16. Shattered Expectations 53

VACATION DISASTERS

17. The Final Straw 59
18. The Cover Story 62
19. A Monstrous Getaway 68

THAT'S UNFORTUNATE

20. Aging Gracefully 75
21. No Pickles Or Olives, Please! 79
22. Imposters 81
23. I'd Like To Slap You 84
24. Honk, Honk Goes 'The Goose Man' 91
25. That Really Stinks! 94

IT JUST DOESN'T FIT

26. You Won't Like Me When I Am Angry 99
27. What The Hell Happened? 101
28. Déjà Vu 104
29. Generated Drama 107

FUNNY CHURCH STUFF

30. That's The Limo? 113
31. Practically Gone With The Wind 116
32. Slap A Bow On It 118
33. Follically Challenged 121
34. A Memorable Entrance 123

WHO IS CALLING ME NOW?

35. Stop Answering The Phone! 127
36. Not Without My Cruise Wear 130
37. They Must Be Dead In A Ditch 133

THEY'RE ALL ANIMALS

38. Just A Warning 137
39. I'm A Star, Dammit 139
40. Tone Down The Sparkles 142
41. Little Liars 145

PERFECTLY TERRIBLE TIMING

42. Guilty Until Proven Innocent 151
43. Woozy 153
44. Body Bags 156
45. Wait, Before You Go... 158
46. It Doesn't Make Sense 160

I WIN, YOU LOSE

47. Damn, I'm Good 165
48. Now That's Competitive 168
49. Better Luck Next Time, Buddy 170

About the Author 173

ACKNOWLEDGMENTS

This book would not have been possible without my husband, Scott, and the silly crap he does. Almost shooting our chicken, the star of another book I am writing, inspired me to write *You're Pretty But Dumb*. Thank you for your love, encouragement, belief in me and for being a constant source of new material for the sequel.

I am so grateful for the very best daughters anyone could have, Victoria and Veronica. I appreciate you reading my stories and giving me feedback even when you both were sick and tired of my so-called 'stupid book.' I especially appreciate the extra help around the house so I could just write.

Thank you to my mom, Linda, for being my biggest cheerleader, the chief of the Grammar Police, and for phenomenal ideas like the 'Pretty But Dumb Bus Tour'. That is going to have to happen; motion sickness be damned.

To Scott's parents, John and Barbara, your contributions were outstanding. We are going to have to start following you around for more stories.

A special thanks to Jessica Verrill of House of Indigo Publishing. Your gentle nudges every few months lit a fire under me to finally write a book. You made the entire process easy, and now I am hooked on writing. My new wake-up time is 4:30 AM.

To my assistant, Michelle, thank you for all of your hard work and enthusiasm.

Finally, to the rest of my family and friends, I appreciate your support.

Love and gratitude to each of you,

Kimberly

DEDICATION

This book is dedicated to:

My husband, Scott, my daughters, Victoria and Veronica, my mother, Linda, my in-laws John, Barbara, Jacqueline, and Barb, my aunt, Gayle, my cousin, Kelly, and the rest of my family and friends who were co-conspirators in mishaps, misunderstandings, embarrassing moments, and in a few instances, foolish behavior.

And a big thank you to the frustrated man at the carnival running the meat-on-a-stick stand who yelled at me, "You're pretty but dumb!" That turned out to be one of the best things anyone ever said to me.

INTRODUCTION

Hey there! Are you ready to laugh your butt off?

For years, my husband has begged me to write about the hilarious things that have happened to me. Luckily, I am the perfect combination of intelligent, funny, and sometimes a little clueless, which add to my charm and are the reason this book was possible.

Between the occasional dumbass behavior of myself and my family members, you'll be able to relate to the embarrassments and mishaps while feeling comforted, knowing that you are not alone.

Finding humor in situations when things go wrong paired with the ability to laugh at your mistakes makes it easier to get through life's challenges, including being repeatedly splashed with feces on Christmas Eve before the guests are due to arrive.

You're Pretty But Dumb is an easy, fun read to lift your spirits, make you laugh aloud, and inspire you to take the bumps in the road of life less seriously. I have also included life lessons at the end of each story. Sure, most are one-liners and not particularly deep, but truthful, nonetheless.

Writing this book and remembering humorous and embarrassing past events and silly disasters has been an absolute joy! My stories will spark your funny memories also. I mean, who hasn't shouted into a poorly placed garbage can when ordering a burger at the drive-thru, am I right?

My best advice is to laugh hard and laugh often. Reading *You're Pretty But Dumb* is a fantastic start!

As a reminder to exercise your funny bone every day, go to www.prettybutdumb.com for 'You're Pretty But Dumb' gear.

Love and laughter,

Kimberly

RIDICULOUS MISUNDERSTANDINGS

Chapter One

YOU'RE PRETTY BUT DUMB

Years ago, my husband, Scott and I went to the Sussex County State Fair with Dave and Tara, our friends. The fair is always in early August, which in NJ means it is so hot and humid that you sweat profusely, even standing motionless in the shade. I am an Autumn/Winter girl, so August is rough for me.

This night was surprisingly cool, breezy, and perfectly comfortable for a change. We went on rides until we could not spin anymore. We watched the smash-up derby, attended the horse show, pet cows, pigs, and goats, and congratulated the blue-ribbon winners. I avoided the llamas, though. They are untrustworthy, and I swear they have it out for me. If a llama has ever spat on you, you understand.

Then it was time to eat! There were so many tasty options. Cheesesteaks, BBQ, blooming onions, funnel cakes, chocolate-dipped frozen cheesecake, and deliciousness were everywhere we looked.

We were all enticed by the smoky aroma coming from the meat-on-a-stick stand. Scott and I wanted beef, and Dave and Tara wanted chicken. I went up by myself while they found a table near the horse show so we could continue to watch.

When I got up to the stand, I told the visibly agitated man that I wanted two chicken and two beef kebobs. He responded roughly, "IT'S PORK."

I said, "Fine. I'll have two chicken and two pork kebobs."

Then he yelled, "IT'S ALL PORK."

I said, "OK, I get it. The meat is 100% pork."

While I was wondering why he was so adamantly stressing the high-quality of the pork, he became furious and yelled, "YOU ARE PRETTY, BUT YOU ARE DUMB." He dragged out the word 'dumb' for emphasis. I would have preferred if he dragged out the word 'pretty' instead.

I could not figure out why he was so mean to me. I assumed the man was exhausted from the crowds and the heat. I awkwardly waited for him to get my order together while he glared at me with utter annoyance.

Typically, I make conversation with people, but he was clearly not in the mood, and I did not like him anyway. When he handed me the four sticks of meat, I timidly asked him, "Which ones are the chicken?"

That last question pushed him beyond his limit of patience. I was sure he wanted to slap me or stab me with one of the nearby skewers. I backed up a little.

He went wild and yelled, "ARE YOU DRUNK OR HIGH?"

I yelled, "NO," right back.

At this point, I just wanted to get away from the man. I walked away mad at the treatment I received and completely confused, looking down at the meat sticks pondering how I would tell them apart? They looked identical.

Then it suddenly hit me. All of them were pork. He only had pork. I started laughing so hard that tears were rolling down my face.

When I got to the table, everyone asked me what had happened. I could hardly breathe or speak through the laughter. As I told Scott and our friends about the mean man at the kebob stand, all four of us were crying from laughing so hard.

All the man had to say was, "We only have pork." I would have understood instantly. In college, I remember my professor saying that 93% of communication is misunderstood. My entire conversation with the angry kebob man was closer to 100%.

Every time I see meat-on-a-stick, I still laugh and hear myself asking, “Which ones are chicken?”

Life Lesson: When ordering food for a group of people, get everyone the same thing.

Chapter Two

YOU'RE GOING TO KILL IT

I am a plant killer. The only plants that survive being in my so-called care are snake plants and spider plants. They are indestructible. If they die, it is because you made a concerted effort to ensure their demise, like setting them on fire or driving over them with your vehicle.

For me, one of the most challenging plants to keep alive are poinsettias. News of my lack of plant rearing skills has spread through the plant world, especially amongst the poinsettia variety.

I can almost hear the internal screams when the unsuspecting flowers see me coming, "Oh no! It's her. She does have the eyes of a killer. Everyone, start drooping, look lifeless, and don't make eye contact!"

The poor things know they are doomed if they come home with me.

However, I do love poinsettias, but nothing I do makes them happy. It is like we need couple's counseling to make a breakthrough in our relationship. When I give them a little water, they drop their leaves and petals. When I give them more water, they still drop their leaves and petals. They baffle me. What do they want?

You can imagine my feelings of inadequacy from the constant bragging by my mother-in-law about her perfect poinsettia. She bought it in early December and placed it in her bay window, where it enjoyed just the right amount of sunlight. Both of my in-laws faithfully watered the remarkable plant and would even argue over the perfect amount of water to give it.

"Johnny, you're going to kill it," my mother-in-law would often yell as he watered.

"Barb, I know what I am doing. We haven't lost a single leaf," he would yell back.

Their poinsettia received the absolute best care and continued to flourish. My in-laws were so proud of themselves for this achievement. Usually, their poinsettias were dead like mine after Christmas and never got to ring in the new year.

Around mid-February, Scott and I stopped to see his parents. We had both been sick and were feeling better, so we were able to visit with them.

They were thrilled to see us and proudly said, "Look at our poinsettia!"

Scott and I stood fifteen feet away from the lush plant that we had heard so much about and had grown envious of, subsequently. We were shocked. We walked closer to examine it. We touched the leaves to confirm what we suspected.

"This is an artificial poinsettia!" Scott said through his laughter.

His parents did not believe him.

"What do you mean? We have been watering it and working so hard to keep it alive."

Scott then pulled the poinsettia out of its pot, revealing the Styrofoam base. His parents were mortified! For three months, they had been arguing over how to best care for their precious poinsettia. My in-laws had to face the truth that they were still poinsettia killers like the rest of us. They did not possess any special poinsettia care secrets. They only knew how to keep a fake plant alive. Anyone could do that.

While we laughed, I inspected their other plants to verify that they were not artificial. The rest were, in fact, real, leaving my in-laws with a shred of dignity. However, they assured us that they will inspect their poinsettias very closely from now on. Scott and I still do not know if we can trust his parents to tell the difference.

Life Lesson: Do not brag about something until you are confident that you have achieved it.

Chapter Three

WHAT DID YOU JUST SAY?

My husband, Scott, is smart, but when speaking, he often phrases common expressions incorrectly. While he is usually only a little bit off, it creates so much confusion. I correct him when I hear it, but occasionally he gets an expression correct, and it throws me through a loop. I start to correct him and then stop mid-sentence, thinking, "Is that how it goes? Is he right?" He has me quite confused after thirty years of marriage.

I especially love when he is having a conversation with someone unaware of his penchant for mangling expressions. At least I am prepared for it. Others are not as fortunate. For instance, when making plans with someone, he suggests, "Let's play it by eye."

I watch the momentary confusion on their faces, and I know just what they are thinking, "OMG, have I been saying this wrong for all of these years?"

Please, they are giving him too much credit. I would never correct him in front of someone, but on the inside, I am yelling, "It's ear, play it by ear." I admit it makes more sense to play it by eye and 'see' what happens, but it is still 'ear,' not 'eye.' The worst part is that 'eye' is starting to sound right to me.

According to Scott, if someone is intelligent, they are sharp as a pin. What? It is tac, sharp as a tac. He never gets that one right. I do not even bother correcting him on that. He still gets the point across accurately, and it is close enough.

The latest expression he has been using is, "We'll see how the worm turns." Yuck, I have never heard that phrase in my life. I do not know what to equate with this. Is he talking about "That's how the cookie crumbles?" Do I need a broom? Am I squishing the worm or sweeping up crumbs? There are too many unanswered questions. I just googled it, and can you believe that "How the worm turns" is an expression? He was right. Do you see my problem here?

I don't even know what to do with, "It's six of one, a dozen of another." You and I know it is really "Six of one, half a dozen of another." It is a comparison of similar things. But Scott has created a math equation instead of a saying. Thanks to my catholic schooling, I admit I have terrible math skills, but this is cruel. OK, so now do we have eighteen of something, or do we have six or twelve? Are we adding, subtracting, dividing, multiplying? Let's throw the baker's dozen into the mix and complicate things even more. Is it now a fraction? Sweet Jesus, help me. What is this man talking about, and why is he so confusing?

My all-time favorite mangled expression of his is, "Hindsight is 50/50." Let's unpack this one. The expression is "Hindsight is 20/20." It is true. When you look at the past, things become so clear, like perfect vision. You would have made better choices if you had the knowledge that you have now back then. In Scott's version, you have a 50/50 chance of it working out. Is this like a raffle? What is the prize? How much are the tickets? I will take five! Wish me luck!!!

Seriously, wish me luck, not only with the 50/50 raffle but with maintaining a firm grasp on the English language; no thanks to Scott. Luckily, my mother is the chief of the grammar police, so I will remain grammatically untarnished no matter how badly Scott twists his words.

. . .

Life Lesson: Do not let anyone make you doubt yourself when you know you are right, especially when they are often wrong.

Chapter Four

WAKE UP, OR I'LL SHOOT

We have nursed Butterscotch, our chicken, back to health four times. We have had numerous chickens over the years but formed such a deep bond with Butterscotch through her rehabilitation stints. The first of which was after a hawk swooped down and grabbed the top of her head, instantly severing her optic nerves and blinding her.

Butterscotch spent four months in the garage recuperating and learning how to find her food and water and walk up and down a ramp before she could rejoin her friends. During that time, she and Scott became particularly close since, in the winter, he worked in his garage daily. He talked to her, and she answered back. It was adorable.

Her most recent health issue rendered her paralyzed. Again, we brought her into the garage to recuperate. She continued to eat and drink and talk to us, so we wanted to give her a chance to recover.

Each morning, I woke up early and rushed down to the garage to make sure Butterscotch survived through the night. I gave her a pill, medicine in a syringe, brought the water up to her beak, picked fresh ryegrass for her, fed her corn, bread, and fresh veggies. I kept her propped up with two pieces of wood wrapped in towels. It was working, and each day, she got a little stronger.

One morning, I slept in, and so did Butterscotch. It was almost a fatal mistake.

Scott went into the garage and saw Butterscotch laying flat on the bottom of the cage with her eyes closed. She opened one eye, looked at him, and then closed it.

Scott thought that it was time to let Butterscotch go. He went to get the pellet gun but, knowing that I would be up shortly, left her there so I could say goodbye. She was such a remarkable chicken and had overcome so many health issues. He left for work very saddened.

Soon after, my phone rang, and it was Scott telling me that Butterscotch had taken her last breath and was gone. I wept for about ten minutes. I had learned so much from this chicken, especially her determination. She even inspired me to write a life coaching book. I was going to miss her terribly.

I went down to the garage and opened the door tentatively. I was surprised that Butterscotch was moving and was still alive! I ran over and propped her up on the rolled-up towels. Her eyes were completely open, shiny, and bright. She talked to me like she did every morning. Butterscotch was ravenous and thirsty.

As I watched her eat, I thought, "OMG, what an idiot!" The chicken had paralysis. She could not move her legs or keep her head up without the rolled-up towels. During the night, she rolled off her towels and could not get up. Scott must have woken her up abruptly. She was still asleep and just opened one eye due to the noise.

I was so ecstatic that my sweet Butterscotch was alive and getting stronger every day. I knew she would recover and get to enjoy her fame as a life-changing chicken in my new book.

From that day on, no one, human or animal, overslept. It was far too risky.

We developed a new warning system at our house for everyone's safety. When anyone heard Scott coming, they had to yell, "Look alive, look alive!"

. . .

Life Lesson: Do not sleep late and never rush to judgment.

Chapter Five

SO, YOU'RE PRESBYTERIAN?

On our way to upstate New York, Scott, the girls, and I stopped at one of our favorite places for lunch. It is an old barn converted into a restaurant. The food tastes homemade, and we always take a package of piping hot cider donuts for the road.

We browsed in the gift shop while waiting to be seated. I found a beautiful pair of dangling silver earrings, and Scott got the last bottle of pine-scented room spray made from essential oils. Finally, our buzzer went off, and we were led to a table by the window with a view of the farm next door.

We perused the tempting options on the menu. We overheard a waiter talking to a couple at the table next to us.

The gentleman asked him, "How is the plant burger?"

The waiter assured him that it was delicious. He was highly animated, and he continued talking, not even pausing to let the couple order. He proudly informed them he was a pescatarian and mainly ate fish and vegetables. He went on and on for five minutes, getting louder and louder with excitement. Everyone within earshot was annoyed. No one wanted to hear about how he prepared his broccoli, what kind of fish was his favorite, and the green juices he made every morning. He was so distracting.

When the waiter stopped talking about his dietary preferences, the gentleman had an opening to speak. With a look of utter confusion on his face, he asked, "So, you're Presbyterian?"

I was sipping my water and almost choked, trying to contain my laughter. When the waiter walked away, the four of us could not stop laughing. The gentleman had to be wondering what the connection was between the waiter's diet of fish and vegetables and his faith.

The overly chatty waiter returned to take our order. After hearing his conversation with the couple next to us, we knew better than to ask any questions. We kept our responses polite and brief while keeping eye contact to a minimum.

Our food arrived and looked delicious as always. Scott, Veronica, and I were pleased with our meals. However, Victoria took a few bites of her fish and chips and decided she did not like it.

I told her, "It's because you are Catholic and not Presbyterian." We all burst out laughing again. I called the pescatarian waiter over and ordered my Catholic girl a juicy burger instead.

Life Lesson: Only order fish and chips at an Irish pub or a seafood joint. Do not encourage overly chatty servers by asking questions or making eye contact.

HOW EMBARRASSING

Chapter Six

'THE ASS MAN'

My husband, Scott, is shy. You can imagine how difficult it was for him years ago when he was having severe ass problems—poor thing.

It all started from bouncing around in his dump truck and backhoe while not getting enough fiber in his diet. He developed painful hemorrhoids and was suffering miserably. If you have experienced hemorrhoid pain, you understand. It is hard to function.

One day, he went to the pharmacy to pick up a prescription. He desperately needed relief. When he entered the pharmacy, at least twenty people were waiting to pick up their prescriptions. The woman at the counter told him his prescription would be ready shortly.

The woman was very unprofessional. She was a pharmacist assistant but was more like an auctioneer calling out ailments and offering the solution to the highest bidder.

"Whose got anxiety? We have got some Zoloft! Step right up! Going, going, gone to the trembling woman in the red dress! Yes, you, ma'am."

Scott was getting increasingly uncomfortable, not just from the hemorrhoids but from the impending embarrassment that he knew was unavoidable.

The shout-outs continued, "Alright, we've got some trouble in the bedroom, don't we? Do not be shy. Come on up. The gentleman in the back who is hiding behind the display of sanitary napkins, you're up. These pills should do the trick. Let us know how it goes, tiger! We are rooting for you! If your erection lasts for more than four hours, call us."

Scott could feel his pulse quicken. His cheeks felt hot; both sets of cheeks now, face and ass. Things were getting intense. He was regretting not taking the pharmacist assistant/auctioneer up on the anxiety pills earlier. He would have outbid that woman in red had he known what was in store for him.

Then it happened.

"Who's got the procto cream? We have relief for you. Who wants to make that anal burning and pain stop?"

Everyone looked around, wondering who it was. Scott could not move, not just because of the hemorrhoids but also the embarrassment of admitting that he was, in fact, 'The Ass Man'.

He quietly slipped out the back door and sent me into the pharmacy instead. I went in and was unashamed to admit that my husband was 'The Ass Man' and retrieved the much-needed procto cream.

Scott had accumulated so much ass gear to make himself more comfortable. He had Preparation H, fiber pills, donut cushions to sit on, stool softeners, Pepto Bismol, and, thanks to me, the procto cream.

Every day, I would watch him when he came home to switch vehicles and had to take his ass gear with him. Add in his allergy paraphernalia, and it was quite a lot of stuff to transfer from vehicle to vehicle.

I had the perfect solution. I suggested Scott take his tool belt and fill it with his ass creams, pills, allergy sprays, and the rest of his anal and nasal products. It would be like the wild west. Instead of drawing a gun, Scott could have total ass and allergy relief at his fingertips.

My other idea was to sew red donut cushions to his pants so he could sit comfortably anywhere he went. The downside was he would look like a baboon.

Scott did not have to take either of my suggestions because the procto cream worked, and he no longer was known as 'The Ass Man'.

Life Lesson: If something is too embarrassing for an in-person purchase, have it delivered in an unmarked box.

Chapter Seven

TOO MUCH JUNK

When my girls were little, my answer for most things was, "Well, they were eating junk food."

It was a twofold victory for me. It was a quick, easy answer to the non-stop questions, and it encouraged healthy eating for my oldest daughter, Victoria, anyway. She was always easy to scare, which made parenting easier.

The younger Veronica was born with street smarts and usually asked for a piece of cake no matter what kind of terrifying story I concocted. It always took way more effort to outsmart her.

One day, I picked the girls up from school. Veronica was two, and Victoria was five. I went to Veronica's classroom, gathered her belongings, and went upstairs to get Victoria. As I put schoolwork into Victoria's backpack, a little boy from Pre-K ran out of the bathroom with his pants down, yelling for help.

Both of my girls looked at him, and I watched as their mouths dropped open. They had never seen the male anatomy and were shocked at the difference. I said nothing and helped them put their coats on.

Once out in the car, Victoria had lots of questions.

I used my go-to response, "Well, the little boy has been eating way too much junk," while hoping it would encourage a healthy after-school snack, like an apple.

Veronica asked for a piece of cake, as usual, but Victoria remained quiet.

I thought I was in the clear because when Victoria asked why Dora the Explorer's head was so big the week before, she accepted my usual response that Dora had been eating way too much junk.

She at once asked with concern, "Is my head too big?"

I assured her that her head was just the right size and suggested she have carrot sticks, which she eagerly ate, giving me such pleasure.

That night, Scott got home from work and got into the shower. I was making dinner and did not notice that Victoria had gone upstairs. She still had questions and was looking for answers. She quietly slipped into the bathroom and secretly peered into the shower. Victoria got quite an eye full. She left the bathroom unnoticed and ran down the stairs to report to me what she found out.

With horror in her voice, Victoria told me, "Daddy has something stuck to his leg!"

Then she reenacted a very girly version of him, lathering his body from head to toe as she shook her hips from side to side and shimmied her shoulders. I was already aware of the thing stuck to his leg, but the feminine lathering dance moves were news to me.

I informed her, "Your father has been eating junk food lately, and now he has to scrub that thing off of his leg." I asked her, "Would you like a pear?"

She took the pear happily and devoured it, recalling what she had seen that day and confirming to herself that junk food was indeed bad for you.

Life Lesson: Lock the damn bathroom door, eat healthy foods, and keep the junk food to a minimum just to be on the safe side.

Chapter Eight

MA'AM, CAN YOU PULL UP FURTHER?

It was three days before Christmas, and I had not purchased any gifts yet. I headed out for a marathon holiday shopping spree with hordes of other last-minute gift-givers. The combination of the intense search for the perfect presents, dense traffic, and painstakingly slow-moving checkout lines drained me.

I rejoiced when I finally had the gifts I needed and headed home. At this point, it was 10:50 PM, and it was freezing outside. I was cold, bone-weary, my feet hurt, and I felt weak and dizzy since I had not eaten since lunchtime. I needed something to eat quickly and pulled into the Burger King parking lot. They closed at 11 PM, so I still had time to order.

As I pulled up to the drive-through, I saw the advertisement for a limited-time item called the Angry Whopper, and I knew it would satisfy my need for nourishment. It was the whopper; only it featured a spicy 'angry sauce', 'angry fried shoestring onions', sliced jalapeños, and the usual lettuce, tomatoes, pickles, and the special mayo.

I was slightly delirious at this point but knew the Angry Whopper was the best solution to my current problem. I pulled up and placed my order, knowing relief was near.

I heard a voice over the speaker say, "Ma'am, can you pull up further? I can't hear you."

Confused, I pulled up much closer to the lit-up menu and repeated my order.

I looked back to understand why I had to repeat my order. I then realized that I was yelling into a garbage can when I placed the order the first time. In my defense, it was extremely dark, I was in a weakened condition from lack of food, and it was a very unusual garbage can. It had a domed lid with a telescopic protrusion that resembled a speaker. The garbage can was placed right next to the advertisement for the scrumptious Angry Whopper but five feet before the actual menu with the speaker.

I pulled up to the drive-through window and realized that I was too tired to be embarrassed. The man at the window tried to make me feel better by telling me people often make the same mistake.

I asked him, "Why don't you just move the weird garbage can?"

He responded, "It's more fun this way!"

He was right. We both laughed as he handed me the burger, and I felt my shame fade away.

One minute later, I was in my driveway. I could not wait another second. I unwrapped the piping hot burger and took a bite. My eyes rolled back in my head. OMG! It was delicious! It was dark, and I could not see what I was eating, but it hit the spot. I felt revived and had the strength to smuggle the packages into my secret hiding spot in the house.

I soon realized I had another problem; I was obsessed with the Angry Whopper, and Burger King was less than a minute from my house. Two days later, I returned to the scene of my embarrassment since I could no longer resist the temptation to have another spicy burger. This time, it was daylight, and I could accurately see the garbage can I had yelled my order into in the darkness the other night.

I laughed, still hearing in my head, "Ma'am, can you pull up further? I can't hear you."

Life Lesson: No 'trash talking'; you'll just embarrass yourself.

Chapter Nine

THE SEX SHOW

When my daughter was in sixth grade, they showed 'the movie'. You know what I am talking about; 'the sex show', albeit tastefully done. The children were separated. The girls learned about the female reproductive system while the boys learned about the male reproductive system. The next day, they switched, and the girls learned about the male reproductive system and the boys, the female reproductive system. Luckily, they saw the movies at the end of the day. The kids were somewhat disgusted, especially the girls. I envisioned the children leaving school in trench coats, hats, and sunglasses while avoiding eye contact.

Later that day, my daughter and I were sitting at the kitchen table, and my husband was making a sandwich. He was raised with two brothers, so he was used to a high testosterone level in his house. Three females dominated our home, and there was only one human male and one sleepy feline male who was not much support for my husband. I took every opportunity to make my husband uncomfortable about girl stuff because I simply loved his reaction.

Then it happened to my delight.

My daughter said, "We saw a movie in school today."

I smiled, knowing what was coming since I signed the consent form from school the week before.

"Really, what was it about?" I asked, knowing full well what was about to happen.

I looked over at my preoccupied husband as he piled more ham onto his sandwich. This was going to be fun!

"The boys have this thing that sticks up and squirts stuff everywhere," she proclaimed with disgust and horror.

I pretended to clutch my non-existent pearls as I brought my hand to my chest with shock and gasped with feigned disbelief and said, "Yuck, that sounds so messy!"

I looked at Scott, who was still clueless as he was cutting his massive sandwich in half. You'd think he would have known what was coming next.

"Scott, has this ever happened to you?" I asked with pretend wonderment.

"Leave me alone. I'm just trying to make a sandwich," he yelled as he blushed.

God, I loved embarrassing him. He took his sandwich and briskly left the room.

Then Victoria got very serious. There was a boy that she liked, and he had a crush on her.

"Do you think John has one of those?" she asked worriedly.

"I am not sure, but it's best to just be friends just in case," I urged her.

Victoria wholeheartedly agreed.

I bought a little more time to prolong her childhood naivety. Later that year, though, she joined the cast of the school play and learned swear words and what a boner was from the eighth graders. Once the boner was out of the bag, so to speak, I could finally use some real swear words, and I had way too much fun with the boner jokes.

Life Lesson: There's nothing wrong with a good boner joke if age-appropriate and well-timed.

Chapter Ten

JERSEY GIRLS DON'T PUMP GAS

I live in New Jersey, the only state besides Oregon where you cannot pump your gas. Thank goodness because I do not know how to use a gas pump, and I don't want to learn either. I have kept my streak alive for fifty-two years and plan to take it to the finish line. I live by a hard and fast rule; Jersey girls do not pump gas, ever.

I have no shame when it comes to sticking to this self-imposed rule. When I am out of state and driving alone, I always forget that it is self-serve and pull up to the pump at the gas station and wait.

I become annoyed, momentarily wondering, "Where the hell is the attendant?"

Then it dawns on me that the attendant is never coming. I know what I must do; I get out of my car and purposely look very perplexed while standing in front of the pump. It works every time—men, women, and I am not ashamed to admit this, even children come to my rescue. I coyly point to my New Jersey license plate and remind them that Jersey girls don't pump gas. We laugh and chit-chat. Everyone is happy, them for doing a good deed but mostly me for keeping the 'no pumping gas' streak alive.

I was coming home late one night and stopped for gas. Only one attendant was working on this busy Saturday night, and five cars were waiting at the pumps. I remembered that my new car's gas tank was on the passenger side and pulled up to an open pump and waited. The attendant was pleasant despite the tired look in his eyes. I asked him to fill it up and handed him my credit card.

Deep in thought, I was brought back to the present time by the click of the pump indicating that my tank was full. The harried attendant heard it also and came to my window and quickly handed me my credit card with the receipt wrapped around it. We thanked each other, and I drove away.

I was exhausted and grateful that my house was about one minute away. I even made the light at the bottom of the hill and was in my driveway before I knew it.

It was so dark in my driveway. Scott must have turned off the lights on the side of the garage. It was OK because my headlights stayed on for thirty seconds and illuminated the path to the back door.

I got ready for bed and felt relieved when I slipped under my goose-down blanket and lay my head on my pillow. I quickly fell into a deep sleep. I am like a cat. I can sleep anywhere, anytime. Scott is so jealous since his mind races and keeps him up.

In the morning, I thought I was dreaming when I heard someone calling my name. I reluctantly opened my eyes and saw that it was 6:30 AM. I heard Scott's voice again. He is an early riser every day, even on Sundays. I could smell the enticing aroma of freshly brewed coffee wafting through the air and decided to get up. I went downstairs quickly, hoping that he did not wake the girls as he kept calling out my name.

"What is it?" I asked with irritation in my voice.

"I have to show you something outside. You are not going to believe it," Scott said, with a mocking smile on his face.

"It is so cold outside. Can't you just tell me what it is? I pleaded.

"No, you have to see this for yourself," he responded.

I slipped into the heels I had on last night, which were right by the back door, and grabbed a sweater. Slightly peeved, I stepped outside into the chilly morning air and followed Scott as he giggled like a schoolgirl and led me to the driveway.

"Where are we going?" I asked impatiently.

Scott stepped out of the way, so I had a clear view of my car.

"OMG!!!!," I exclaimed.

"So, I see you got gas last night, huh?" Scott teased.

To my horror, the gas pump handle and hose were still attached to my gas tank. Scott laughed.

I was mad at first. "That was not my fault!" I yelled. I have the receipt. The attendant gave me back my credit card and walked away. It is his fault, clearly."

Scott laughed even harder. "I can't wait to share this with the guys at work tomorrow. I always have the best wife stories," he proudly proclaimed.

He was right, and I always have the best husband stories. We both laughed, knowing we were a perfect match.

Life Lesson: Always check your side mirrors to ensure you are not attached to the gas pump when you pull away. Buy a car with the gas tank on the driver's side.

Chapter Eleven

CONFUSION AND DISGUST

It was Palm Sunday, a week before Easter, and there was standing room only due to the members of the congregation who only attended mass on or near holy days.

Our priest, Father Ray, stood in front of the altar holding a wooden cross with Jesus on it. He invited everyone to form two lines and come forward, but he did not describe what we should do when we reached the front of the line. Then Father Frank joined him, also holding a wooden cross with Jesus on it.

Starting from the first pews on the left and right sides of the aisle, the congregation members began forming two lines. As each person stood in front of the priests, they bent down and did something, but I was not sure what. I got in line behind my uncle, John Paul. My grandmother was behind me. I asked her what we were supposed to do, but she did not answer me. John Paul, who was nine years older than me and acted more like my brother, turned around and responded to my question. Being just ten years old, I was not suspicious as he smiled back at me with such delight in his big brown eyes.

John Paul was next. He bent down, did what he was supposed to do, and moved to the side, watching and waiting with anticipation.

It was my turn. I waited as Father Ray wiped the foot of Jesus with a white cloth. Feeling a little uneasy, I bent down and followed my uncle's instructions. I stuck my tongue out as far as I could and licked the foot of Jesus.

Father Ray looked at me with confusion and disgust as he vigorously wiped Jesus's foot. My face felt hot as I looked over at the person in front of the other line next to me. Then I understood. I was supposed to kiss the foot of Jesus, not lick it. I made eye contact with John Paul, who laughed without making a sound. I rushed back to my seat, completely embarrassed and hoping my friends from school did not see what I had done.

For the next week, John Paul reminded me of my embarrassing mistake by licking objects and laughing. He grew tired of this and went back to his favorite way of tormenting me, which was chasing me, catching me, and farting on me.

Life Lesson: Always consider the source when you receive guidance. Never lick anything if someone else had their mouth on it, even if it was wiped with a special white cloth by a man of the cloth.

Chapter Twelve

A TRAIL OF DESTRUCTION

When my mother was moving, she asked me to help her pack her clothing, shoes, hats, and purses, which was not a small feat. This woman loves to shop and always buys only high-quality clothing and accessories. When she finds an item she likes, she purchases it in every color available.

My mom is extra excited if something is reversible. Whenever I get a new article of clothing, she asks, “Is it reversible?”

Even if I say “No,” she makes me put it on inside out to see if it could be reversible.

Going through her closet, she found three pairs of wedge sandals that she had never worn. They were gorgeous. Of course, she had them in bright red, white, and tan suede. She added the three pairs of shoes to my pile for me to take home.

I had the shoes in my closet for a couple of years and forgot I had them. One day, I was cleaning out my closet and came across them. The warm weather was coming soon, and I was excited to wear them.

A couple of weeks later, Scott needed to go to Walmart for motor oil for his truck and asked if I would come with him. I went upstairs to get dressed, and since it was a warm day, I selected the suede tan wedge sandals with cropped jeans and a white summer top. The wedges were so comfortable due to the very thick heels, even though they were high.

Once in Walmart, Scott and I headed towards the most boring aisle of all, the motor oil and filter aisle. As I was walking, my right shoe felt like it had a pebble stuck in the sole, making every step feel wobbly. When we made it to the motor oil area, I looked at the bottom of my shoe. I was shocked to see that the sole of the wedge heel and a deep crack down the center from side to side, and part of the sole was missing. The left shoe also felt funny, and I noticed that it had the same crack as the right shoe, which was odd because no one ever wore the sandals, and they were fine when I left my house.

I walked up and down the aisle, helping Scott find his truck's correct oil and filter. As I walked, I noticed pieces of the rubber wedge heels breaking off from both of my shoes. It was getting harder to walk. We finally found what Scott needed and were ready to head to the register to checkout. I took five more steps, and even bigger chunks of the bottom of my shoes broke off.

I told Scott, "I have a problem. The bottoms of my shoes are crumbling. I will never make it to the register. I might be able to make it to the shoe department, though."

I carefully walked towards the shoe department, leaving a trail of black rubber chunks behind me with each step. The remaining part of the soles of my shoes was so uneven that I could hardly walk. I tried walking on my tippy toes for the last stretch. Finally, we made it. I sat down and sent Scott to pick out a pair of shoes since I certainly could not do it.

He brought me one ugly pair after another.

Disappointed, I said, "Let me look."

There was nothing good; he was right. Suddenly, I spotted a pair of black platform heels in faux suede. I walked back to my chair and made it just in time. Both shoes simultaneously imploded and disintegrated into a pile of broken pieces of rubber.

Thank God the black platforms fit and were cute enough. I picked up the remaining pieces of my wedge sandals, which at that point consisted of the ankle straps and little scraps of suede, and put them into the shoebox the platforms came in. My new shoes felt fabulous. As we left the shoe aisle, we looked back at the remains of my shoes scattered all over the floor. We were shocked by the mess.

At the register, I half expected to be swarmed by security. What happened was so odd and suspicious-looking. I was hoping that the employees did not think we were stealing.

No one asked any questions, and I walked out of Walmart with structurally sturdy shoes.

Although never worn, I suspected that the shoes were older than my mother thought, and the rubber got brittle and broke apart as I wore them.

When I got home, I immediately threw out both the red and the white wedge sandals. I was never going to leave a trail of destruction behind me again.

Life Lesson: It is not easy walking in someone else's shoes; sometimes, it is downright impossible.

HOLIDAYS AND MISHAPS

Chapter Thirteen

MERRY EFFIN' CHRISTMAS

What was that strange sound? I ran into the bathroom next to the kitchen and heard the odd gurgle again. I screamed as the water suddenly overflowed from the toilet rushing over my bare feet, and began pouring into the kitchen. My only consolation was that the water was clean, warm, and soapy. But still, yuck!

My husband came running in and knew we had a big problem. My daughter was taking a shower upstairs, and the water backed up.

Now it was making sense. Earlier, when I opened the washing machine in the basement, water poured out onto the floor. I assumed something was wrong with the washing machine. Unfortunately, it was more serious; something was wrong with the septic.

It was Christmas Eve, and we were getting ready for our guests to arrive. We were about to start preparing the shrimp, scallops, salmon, and the rest of the delicious food we planned to serve.

I was not ready for the actual shitshow that was about to be unleashed on my favorite holiday.

We hurried down to the basement, and Scott took the cap off the septic pipe that leads outside. He needed something long to push into the line to see if there was a blockage. He remembered a long flexible tube that our neighbor had left in the woods behind our house. It was pouring rain and dark, but Scott returned triumphantly with it.

He started feeding the long wet, muddy tube into the septic pipe. My job was to hold the other end of the filthy, slippery tube. Tensions were high, extremely high, as anyone who has helped their husband with a project that is not going well can relate.

Scott started shoving the tube into the septic pipe with such force as he yelled, "Merry... Effin'... Christmas..." with each thrust interspersed with "You're not holding the tube right!"

Mud, shit, and slime splashed all over the walls, floors, and both of us.

I knew it would be funny to him later, much later, but in the meantime, my body shook as I held in my laughter.

Scott figured out the problem. The pipe had collapsed outside just before the septic. There was nothing we could do until the morning. We had to call off our Christmas Eve party. Everyone insisted on coming still, but Scott was not in a good mood, and we could not use the water, flush the toilets, and did not want our guests peeing outside behind the shed.

Scott, our two daughters, and I still had a great Christmas Eve, and he was able to laugh about the shitty situation.

Early on Christmas Day, Scott dressed up like the Gorton's fisherman in his yellow slicker, pants, and boots. Like an angry hero dressed in yellow rubber from head to toe, I watched as he slowly disappeared into the bowels of the septic. I quietly took pictures from behind the bushes, still shaking from laughter.

He yelled, "I see you taking pictures!"

I kept snapping away as I giggled.

A bit later, he emerged crud-covered yet victorious after repairing the pipe. Then we had to deal with the other problem. What were we going to do with so much fish leftover from Christmas Eve?

. . .

Life Lesson: Even a holiday that starts out shitty can turn out better than expected.

Chapter Fourteen

MORE SHRIMP DIP, ANYONE?

I am still not sure what happened. Scott and I are both excellent cooks, typically. We were excited to host Christmas Eve and planned a delicious menu with various appetizers, seafood, salads, and decadent desserts.

Scott's family only eats seafood on Christmas Eve; no meat is allowed all day. Scott claims it is a religious rule and must be adhered to no matter what. I always find humor in this because his family is not very churchy, yet they cling to this holiday rule as if you will burn in hell for all of eternity if meat even touches your lips on this holy day. Scott and I still argue about this every year. We are of the same religion and are both of Polish descent. Refraining from eating meat on Christmas Eve is a tradition his family follows. It has nothing to do with religion. But I go along with it for the Christmas Eve meal. Although one year, I accidentally served pigs in a blanket, and everyone happily ate them, forgetting about their no meat rule.

My father whispered to me, "I thought no meat was allowed?

It did not even occur to me, but I secretly felt vindicated as I watched Scott and his family thoroughly enjoy the meat. I mean, how much fish can someone eat in one day?

During the day of Christmas Eve, it is a different story. My oldest daughter and I sneak out for big burgers. It is not because I am being rebellious; it's just that I am so weak by the time Christmas Eve rolls around. I have been shopping, decorating, cleaning, wrapping presents, and so busy that we order pizza on the nights leading up to the holiday. By Christmas Eve, I need meat to give me the strength for the final push for holiday entertaining.

My family, on the other hand, always had beef on Christmas Eve. Sauerbraten was one of our favorites. I would think about it all year long, the way the tender meat soaked up the rich spiced gravy and gently kissed the potato dumplings. The red sweet and sour cabbage always provided just the right twang to the meal.

This Christmas Eve, Scott planned to prepare pistachio-crusted salmon with raspberry chipotle sauce, lump crab cakes, garlic mashed potatoes, cheesecake, chocolate peanut butter pie topped with fresh whipped cream, and molasses crinkle cookies.

I decided to make new dishes and turned to my trusted cookbook that I had gotten at a garage sale years ago, called *The Cooking Affair*. Everything I made from that cookbook was always fabulous. I had no fear of making something for guests that I had never prepared before.

Since Scott had the main meal and dessert covered, I planned to make fresh bruschetta, garlic crostini, Cajun coleslaw to accompany the crab cakes, shrimp balls, broccoli cheese bites, red pepper hummus, and spinach dip in a bread bowl. Easy, right?

I went to the supermarket and gathered my ingredients the day before so everything would be fresh. Having already snuck out for my power burger on the pretense of running to CVS, I was ready to cook. I started with the bruschetta. I had the exact ingredients, which is unusual since I am the Queen of substitution. I can make a dish without the main ingredient. Most of the time, my creative swaps work out.

I mixed the ingredients and added the parmesan cheese last. The cheese was a different brand than what I usually buy. It was so odd; it did not meld with the rest of the ingredients. Instead, it formed little hard clumps and was unpleasant texture-wise. I eyed the food processor on the counter and buzzed the bruschetta, thinking I was so innovative. Unfortunately, instead of bruschetta, I now had a tomato smoothie. No big deal, I would just run out later and get jarred bruschetta.

Next, I opened the package of shrimp and, to my disgust, gagged from the vile stench that emanated from them. I had to go back to the store anyway for bruschetta and would get new shrimp.

At the supermarket, the man behind the fish counter told me that the three pounds of shrimp I had bought twelve hours earlier simply spoiled on my ride home. Since I live less than a minute from the store, I informed him that it was impossible and demanded fresh, unspoiled shrimp that were not so damn fragile that they could not handle being unrefrigerated for two minutes.

With my new sturdy shrimp and jar of bruschetta, I headed home. I decided to make the coleslaw first, so it had time to marinate. I make fantastic coleslaw; I am talking award-winning. But I decided to follow a new recipe instead. It was awful, almost slimy. I put it into the refrigerator, hoping it would improve by dinner.

Now, I was ready to make the shrimp balls. These were going to be fantastic! I put the beautiful shrimp in the food processor and hit the pulse button.

"Is it supposed to be this soupy?" I said to myself aloud.

I could not get the shrimp to form balls.

Scott walked in and asked. "What did you do? You ruined three pounds of shrimp!"

"It will be fine," I assured him. "I will just make it into a shrimp dip and serve it with crackers."

I went completely rogue and added what I thought would tighten the liquid shrimp up to create a dip-like consistency. I put my strange concoction into the fridge next to my slippery coleslaw.

Next up was the red pepper hummus. I had never made it before and added too much tahini paste. I was not pleased. I threw it out.

It was time to make the broccoli bites. The consistency was just right, and the dough formed nice little balls. Whew, at least that went well.

I was exhausted, the kitchen was a wreck, and the garbage can was full of my prior disastrous attempts for my portion of the meal.

I decided to run back to the store to buy the spinach dip since I was going back anyway for hummus and some new coleslaw just in case mine did not improve during the marination process.

I came home with my store-bought hummus, spinach dip, and coleslaw. Since I had finished destroying and repurchasing my contribution to the holiday menu, I asked Scott if he needed any help.

"Just get out of the kitchen now and don't touch anything I am making," Scott said.

Secretly, I was relieved and went into the living room to fluff the pillows on the couch and pick up any ornaments the cats knocked off the tree.

It started to snow as the guests were arriving! Our friends Dave, Tara, their daughter, Jocelyn, and her seven-year-old daughter, Alexis, came to the door with Alaskan crab legs and their homemade wine. My parents brought seafood salad and creamy lobster bisque soup.

I put out my jarred bruschetta, pre-packaged hummus, and store-bought spinach dip with garlic crostini, crackers, a raw veggie platter, assorted cheeses, and my failed shrimp balls, which I creatively turned into a seafood dip. Everyone was hungry and dug in.

I sat next to Jocelyn, and served her the odd shrimp mixture. She took a bite and did not say anything. I asked her how it was, and she said that it was good and changed the subject. When I offered her more shrimp dip, she politely declined.

"I'll send you home with some," I told her.

Jocelyn gave me a weak smile.

I was back and forth from the kitchen to the living room, refreshing drinks and taking empty plates. I noticed that my so-called shrimp dip was practically untouched.

I heard laughter upon returning to the living room and entered unnoticed.

I heard Scott say, "I wanted to put name cards on the dishes I made, but it wasn't necessary because the food I prepared was in solid form, and Kim's dishes were just smooth pastes. She could have served her entire meal in a four-sectioned dip dish. She destroyed everything she touched, and I finally threw her out of the kitchen."

Everyone looked up and saw me, at once becoming quiet. I started laughing, and everyone joined me.

We had a fantastic night full of delicious food, family, friends, and roaring laughter at my cooking mishaps, making the night even more memorable.

Right before everyone left, I opened the refrigerator door and gasped. I forgot to serve my broccoli bites.

"Who wants broccoli bites to take home? I offered.

No one responded. Everyone quickly put on their coats, thanked us for a beautiful evening, and ran away without my broccoli bites. Who could blame them?

Curious, I popped them into the oven and tried one when they finished baking. I offered one to Scott, he refused. I took a bite and, without saying a word, threw the entire tray into the garbage.

It was the funniest Christmas Eve celebration we ever had, thanks to my horrendous cooking. Scott still forbids me from helping with the

Christmas Eve cooking. I merely sneak out for a burger and fluff the pillows.

Life Lesson: You cannot hide your cooking mistakes by liquifying everything in a food processor. Everyone will notice, trust me.

Chapter Fifteen

TURKEY WARS

Sometimes there is an unspoken competition about who is more skilled in the kitchen, the mother-in-law or her precious son's new wife. For some daughters-in-law, it can get intense, especially around the holidays.

My mother-in-law despises cooking turkey. She is overly concerned it will not be moist enough. No one wants a dry turkey, no matter how much gravy is available. She tried everything in the quest for the most succulent turkey, such as injecting the bird with marinade, using an oven bag to keep it juicy, and brining. One year, our cousin, Todd, even deep-fried the turkey while trying not to burn down the deck and the house.

After every Thanksgiving, as we clean up, my mother-in-law always whispers, "Was the turkey moist?"

I always assured her that it was very moist, even on the few occasions when it was slightly dry.

I am never involved in making a turkey for the holidays. I bring side dishes like my grandmother's sausage stuffing, homemade cranberry sauce, and my much-in-demand cucumber salad. The cucumber salad is a big hit.

My nephew, John, always asks, "Aunt Kim, is it OK if I drink the left-over dressing in the bowl?"

Having people ask if they can drink my salad dressing always makes me happy, and I say, "Of course, go for it."

Scott loves to bake and brings one of his fabulous desserts, like a three-tiered celebration cake, a pumpkin pie made from scratch with home-grown pumpkins, or his creamy rice pudding with fresh whipped cream.

When my sister-in-law, Jacqueline, joined the family, she was so sweet in offering to make the turkey for Granny. Jacqueline knows her way around a turkey. I was impressed as I watched her massage the turkey with butter and seasonings under the skin. Her turkey was exquisite. I was not sure if this pleased my mother-in-law or not.

The following year, extra guests were coming to Thanksgiving, and we needed two turkeys. Jacqueline volunteered to make one of the turkeys.

I decided to stir the proverbial turkey pot. It was purely for fun, and I have a warped sense of humor. I told Jaqueline that Pa was making a turducken, a decadent fowl concoction involving a turkey stuffed with a duck stuffed with a chicken.

Not to be outdone, Jacqueline proclaimed with a competitive spirit, "That's it, I am deboning the turkey and making roll-ups with my grandmother's chestnut stuffing."

Of course, I immediately informed Granny and Pa of Jaqueline's plans, and Granny ordered the five-star QVC gourmet marinated turkey breasts. I instigated quite a battle that the whole family would benefit from selfishly.

On Thanksgiving, the entire family gathered around the table and had the most delicious meal with two supremely moist turkey options, divine side dishes, and yummy desserts.

While cleaning up, Granny whispered, "Was my turkey moister than Jackie's?"

As always, I told her. "Yes, it was."

When Granny left the room, I said to Jacqueline, "That was the best turkey I have ever had."

Jacqueline was delighted, and I effortlessly set the stage for next year's turkey wars.

Life Lesson: Creating friendly competition in the kitchen benefits everyone.

Chapter Sixteen

SHATTERED EXPECTATIONS

It was our first Christmas Eve in our new house. Both Scott's and my family were coming.

There was snow on the ground, our tree looked beautiful despite the kitten repeatedly knocking off the ornaments, and we had a roaring fire in the family room. It felt so snuggly.

I was slightly overwhelmed with so many guests coming, so my mom came early to help us get ready for the party. My mother loves to entertain, and being a perfectionist, she takes it very seriously. I remember one year when my mom was hosting her first Easter with my stepfather. He had a huge family. We were expecting seventy people after mass at 2 AM.

My cousin, Kelly, slept over, and the two of us baked Greek desserts for three days straight. We had never made these recipes before, and for one of the cookies, we used margarine instead of butter. According to my mom, they were delicious but not authentic enough. She insisted we make a new batch. Kelly and I were exhausted, but we did it. After, we collapsed on the floor, covered in flour, slightly delirious and giggling.

When my mom arrived to help me with my party, I had everything under control. I just needed help getting the appetizers ready. My mother had more important things to do first to ensure the party was a success. She conducted a thorough walk-through and fluffed pillows, adjusted the pictures on the wall ¼ of an inch, and created just the perfect mood lighting in each room. I let her do her thing until I heard her call up from the basement.

"There's an area under the stairs that could use some touch-up with a little paint," she said with concern.

I took a big sip of wine before I responded, "Just get up here! No one is going under the stairs in the basement. Help me make a veggie platter."

After five more minutes of doing something unnecessary in the basement, she came upstairs to help me in the kitchen. When we finished, she had a great idea.

"Let's make hot mulled cider. You have the ingredients, and it will smell so inviting when the guests arrive. The cups from your antique punch bowl set will be perfect for serving it in," she suggested.

As the cider heated up on the stove, the spicy scent of cinnamon, cloves, and sweet apples and oranges filled the kitchen.

When the guests arrived, the first thing they all asked was, "What is that delicious smell?"

They were all looking forward to the warm cider on a wintry night. Everyone gathered around my mother at the stove with anticipation as she gave the cider one last stir.

There was an excited collective, "Ooooooo."

She reached for an antique crystal cup and, while holding it over the pot, ladled the hot liquid into it. Instantly, the cup disappeared with a crash of broken glass into the bottom of the pot. My mother stood there with only the handle of the cup in her hand.

There was a sad collective, "Uuuuggghhh!"

My mother dropped the handle into the pot, pushed it to the back of the stove, and diverted everyone's attention with, "Who wants some fabulous shrimp puffs?"

Again, there was an excited collective, "Ooooooo," and the cider disaster no longer mattered.

Life Lesson: When something goes wrong, pivot and offer everyone shrimp to distract them from the mishap.

VACATION DISASTERS

Chapter Seventeen

THE FINAL STRAW

When I was nine, my mom and I went to the Great Gorge Resort with her boyfriend for a long weekend. Let me tell you; it felt like it was a month.

Patrick was in his fifties, and his children were adults. He was not interested in dealing with a young child at this point in his life. He was having a midlife crisis. Patrick had a corvette, a beautiful young blonde girlfriend, and a passion for disco. I did not fit into this picture; hell, I hardly fit into his corvette. There was no seat for me, and I had to sit on a pillow on top of the emergency brake. Talk about cramping his style. When my mother was not around, he and I would glare at each other with disdain.

The first day we arrived at the resort, I entered a backgammon contest. It was for adults, but there were no rules barring children from entering. The judges and the rest of the contestants did not see me as a threat until I made it to the final round after beating six adults. My mother was proud, but Patrick was annoyed that I had made it that far and got so much attention. I would have won the whole competition, but the man I was playing against was gruff. To the judges ' relief, I became flustered and made an error that cost me the game and the prize. Presenting a nine-year-old with a complimentary romantic weekend at the resort just felt so inappropriate.

That night, Bob Hope was the headliner, and we saw his show. It was excellent! He stayed right down the hall from us, and I staked out his hotel room and got his autograph. That was the last time I had fun that weekend, thanks to Patrick, although I did get the last laugh in the end.

Patrick had plans for me for the rest of the trip, convincing my mother that I would have fun. Each morning, he happily dropped me off at the resort camp. He was so thrilled that I would be occupied and out of sight that he was practically skipping on the way to camp.

I, on the other hand, did everything I could to escape. One morning a little girl threw up sliced peaches. I offered to go back to my room and get towels. Of course, I had no intention of returning. The camp counselor saw through my attempt for freedom and quickly rejected my offer. I tried faking a stomachache, a headache, amnesia, but the counselors were not falling for it. Patrick poisoned them against me, obviously.

Even at dinner, I had to eat with the camp kids. The children's dining area was a dark, windowless wood-paneled room while the adults ate in a ballroom filled with music, laughter, and an abundance of natural light.

One night, when the counselors had their backs turned, I darted out of the bad place and ran into the ballroom, searching for my mother. When I found her, she was overjoyed to see me, but Patrick just glared at me. I returned the sentiment.

Moments later, the counselors found me and tried to remove me from the ballroom.

My mother said, "Let her stay."

As usual, Patrick was visibly irritated by me, but my mom and I had an enjoyable time. After dinner, we went back to our room. I got ready for bed, but Patrick wanted to go dancing and show off his John

Travolta moves and his fake tan. My mother was uncomfortable leaving me and told me to lock the door and not open it for anyone. After they left, I chained the door in addition to locking it. I got into bed and fell fast asleep.

When Patrick and my mother returned from the discotheque, they could unlock the door but could not open it due to the chain. They yelled my name, banged on the door, and called the phone on the nightstand next to me. I heard them, but just for spite, I pretended to be asleep.

Patrick had to call maintenance to cut the chain, and I continued to act like I was sleeping. I was impressed with my award-winning performance. The following day, my mother told me how I slept through the noise. For my second act, I portrayed shock, and my mom believed me. However, Patrick had his suspicions—rightfully so.

I was expecting Patrick to whisk me off to camp, but instead, we left a day early, and he drove us home. The weekend at Great Gorge was the final straw that ended the relationship between my mom and Patrick. I never saw him again or went to day camp. My mother and I were delighted.

Life Lesson: Bring a spiteful child with you on a romantic weekend getaway if you want to end an already strained relationship.

Chapter Eighteen

THE COVER STORY

Our worst beach vacation was when Veronica was two and Victoria was five. Since we were still neck-deep in the 'toddler gear' stage, I found a hotel right on the beach. From the pictures, it looked lovely and very convenient. There was one bedroom, a kitchen, and a living room with something called a duo bed. I was unsure what that was since the description was vague, but it was a bed or perhaps two beds. There was also a pool, grills for the guests, and a fun outdoor bar area with live music.

When I checked in, the woman at the reservation desk was not very warm and fuzzy but nice enough. She gave me the key. Scott, the girls, and I went to the room, bringing as much of our luggage as possible. When I opened the door, I did not see a bed. There was just an "L" shaped couch with a thick grey vinyl cover with a floral design.

"Oh, no! Is that the duo bed?" I said aloud.

The door was still open, a maintenance man passing by responded. "Yep, that's the duo bed," he said.

"How does this work?" I asked.

"It's simple, you sit on it like a couch, and when you want to go to sleep, you just lie down," he said, seemingly enormously proud of this so-called bed.

"What about that vinyl cover? Do you take it off when done sitting and want to sleep?" I asked.

"Never," he said adamantly.

"What are you hiding under the cover, bloodstains?" I joked.

His demeanor shifted from friendly to stern as he repeated, "Never remove the cover."

Ok," I assured him as he looked at me with distrust in his eyes and then left before giving me one more cold glare.

"That was strange," I said to Scott.

He agreed and went back to the car to get the rest of our stuff.

I got the girls into their bathing suits and gathered our chairs, towels, sunscreen, water, snacks, sand toys, and the rest of the beach paraphernalia. Our hotel was on the water, but it was still a long walk since the beach was vast, especially for Scott since he had to carry Veronica, the chairs, and the heavy cooler bag.

We found just the right spot close enough to the water without being in danger of our stuff getting wet when the high tide rolled in.

I spread the blanket, put up the umbrella, and opened the chairs. Scott is not a beach person. He works in the sun and the heat every day, and the beach is the last place he wants to be.

Scott just sat down, and the second his butt hit the chair, Veronica said, "I want to go back to the room and watch *Scooby-Doo*."

Scott put Veronica over his shoulder without saying a word, and they walked back to the room.

Victoria and I stayed and had fun boogie boarding. We waited for Scott and Veronica to return, but they never did. That meant we had to carry everything back to the room ourselves. Ugh.

When we walked into our hotel room, I gasped.

"Scott! Did you remove the cover from the duo bed? What have you done?"

"I had to. I wanted to take a nap. I was sweating, lying on top of the vinyl cover. It was like sleeping in a diner booth. It's pretty comfortable now, and there were no bloodstains," Scott said as he laughed.

"OK," I said with unease remembering the adamant warning from the strict maintenance man. "I'm surprised that an alarm did not sound the moment the cover was removed, alerting the swat team to swarm, swarm, swarm!"

I looked at the cover on the floor. It was so stiff, making it impossible to fold, and it engulfed five feet of floor space we could not spare.

I went back outside and saw that the housekeeper was still on our floor. She looked friendly.

I took a chance and asked casually, "If ever I needed to remove the vinyl cover from the duo bed, would you be able to put it somewhere? It is extremely uncomfortable for sleeping."

"I wouldn't take it off," she warned in a hushed voice, "but if you absolutely must, it has to stay in your room."

"Ok, thanks," I said, relieved that she did not blow a whistle and have me taken to a backroom for 'reprogramming' so I would be accepting of the vinyl cover like the rest of the well-behaved Stepford guests.

A little later, we decided to go to the boardwalk, which was about half a mile away. When we left the room, we passed the prior friendly housekeeper, who now just glared at us with narrowed eyes.

We caught the maintenance man watching us with disdain from the supply room under the stairs.

When we were out of earshot, I said to Scott, "That was creepy."

We stopped by the car to get the double stroller that I purchased for the trip. Veronica did not like being contained in any way, but I figured she would be happy not to have to walk so much. I was wrong, Veronica wanted to walk, but Victoria insisted on being in the stroller. It took a while, but we made it to the rides, ate tornado fries, frozen custard, and headed back to the hotel room.

The boardwalk was very crowded now. Veronica refused to get into the stroller but insisted on pushing it. If we helped her at all, she freaked out and went back ten steps and started over. The walk back took an excessive amount of time, and Victoria became tired and wanted to be in the stroller. Hell, I wanted to be in the stroller myself.

Because it was too heavy now, Veronica could not push the stroller and demanded that her sister get out. Scott scooped up the little screamer, put her over his shoulder, and we picked up the pace and power walked back to our room.

As we walked up the stairs to our room, we passed another housekeeper whom we had never seen before. She stared at us disapprovingly until we were out of sight. We caught a different maintenance man glaring at us from the end of the hall as we unlocked our door.

Once safely inside our room, I asked Scott, "What is wrong with these people? The maintenance man must have poisoned the whole staff against us because we don't like the duo bed, and now they hate us. I am a little scared. Should we put the cover back on? I feel like they know we removed it. Were they in our room?"

Scott said, "There is no way I am sleeping on vinyl. The cover stays off!"

"OK," I said, feeling uneasy. "We are staying in the friggin' 'Bates Motel. Sleep with one eye open, and no one is taking any showers!" I told him.

The next day, we decided to go crabbing. As we walked to our car, every staff member we passed looked at us with contempt.

"OMG, they do hate us all because you took that damn cover off," I yelled at Scott.

I forgot about our popularity troubles once we reached the dock. Scott baited our crab traps with raw chicken and lowered them into the water. We watched cheerfully so the crabs would feel safe before we killed them, unlike the threatening way the staff at the Bates Motel glared at us with whatever they had planned.

"I want to go back to the room and watch *Scooby-Doo*," Veronica predictably insisted.

Scott put her over his shoulder and went back to the room. Of course, Victoria and I caught a crab when Scott drove off to watch another episode of *Scooby-Doo*. And not the original ones either, but the crappy spin-off version, *Scooby Kids*. I felt sorry for him until I realized we had caught a bunch of crabs. Now what?

Fearing our screaming would scare off the crabs, a man on the dock helped us. When Scott and Veronica returned, we had a whole bucket full of fresh crabs for dinner.

We dropped off the crabs at our room and headed to the beach. This time, the coast was clear, and we did not see the wannabe Norman Bates maintenance man or the staff members whom he trained to loathe us.

Minutes later, my phone rang. It was the woman at the front desk. She asked if we would mind switching rooms since they had a booking issue. I was afraid to refuse, so I agreed in hopes that this kind gesture would make the staff stop glaring at us with such hatred.

The woman thanked me but lacked sincerity and told me she would call me when our new room was ready.

We enjoyed ourselves at the beach, and luckily, Veronica was happy, so Scott got to relax. I kept checking my phone to see if our new room was ready because I needed time to pack our stuff, but still, there was no call.

We decided to head back to the room after a couple of hours. When we got to our floor, I could see our door was open. Norman Bates was there with two angry-looking housekeepers.

"OMG! They saw the duo bed cover on the floor! Their suspicions were confirmed. In their judgmental eyes, we were terrible people," I thought, feeling uncomfortable.

"I thought that you were going to call me so I could pack our things?" I asked, acting brave.

Unapologetically, Norman said, "We are moving your things to another room because we have to get it ready for the new guests right now."

"I'll finish it myself," I told him. "I've had enough of this!"

We packed quickly and checked out, fearing for our safety. As we drove away, the eerie hotel staff watched us with disapproval.

Life Lesson: Never believe anyone's cover story.

Chapter Nineteen

A MONSTROUS GETAWAY

Scott fertilized twenty lawns for his clients before leaving for our long weekend in Lake Placid, NY. As we were driving, Scott was complaining about his eyes burning. He thought it was his allergies. His eyes became increasingly scratchy and swollen, and Scott was having a hard time keeping them open. He took his allergy medicine and waited for relief as we drove through the pouring rain.

We finally arrived at our hotel that was supposed to be on the water. Our room was the furthest point possible from the water. The only window was like a porthole. To see the water, you had to stand on the balcony on your tippy-toes to just barely see the water through the trees—certainly nothing like the picture I saw when booking.

It was late. We had just driven five hours in the rain. We were too tired to go out to eat, so we got takeout from the restaurant across the street. The food was OK.

We went to bed looking forward to the fun things we would do the next day. In the morning, Scott's eyes were even more swollen. He put in eye drops and asked me to drop him off at his secret fishing spot forty-five minutes away in the middle of nowhere. Usually, I don't enjoy driving because there is so much traffic where we live. But here, the winding roads were quiet, and the scenery of the mountains, wildflowers, and rivers was so serene that I did not mind the long drive.

I dropped my puffy-eyed husband off on the side of a mountain road that had such a high elevation; it felt like it was on top of the world. He told me to come back to this very spot in three hours. I watched as he disappeared through the trees carrying his fishing gear. He was so thrilled. He loves fishing.

I decided to go shopping in town. I leisurely snooped in the antique shops, bought handmade pine-scented soap, and admired the beautiful pottery lovingly made by local artists. I stopped at the bakery that made the best snickerdoodles and ordered one and a big cup of coffee with extra cream. I enjoyed them by the lake. The breeze was gentle, and the sun broke through the clouds and shone on the lake, making it sparkle like diamonds. The sound of the water lapping on the shore relaxed me even further.

Time went by too fast, and it was time to pick up Scott. I hopped in my car, rolled down the windows, and blasted Shania Twain, which was the perfect choice since I loved her music, and she grew up not far from Lake Placid.

I made it back to the mountain road, but I did not see Scott. I kept driving, wondering if I was in the wrong spot. Everything looked the same suddenly. Finally, I turned around, thinking I must have gone too far. There was no cell service, and I was starting to get worried that something had happened to him.

I kept driving, and then I saw something off in the distance. As I got closer, I realized it was Scott. He was running towards me. I stopped, and he jumped into the car out of breath. His eyes were even puffier from when I saw him hours earlier, and he was pissed.

"You drove right past me way back there. I was standing there on the side of the road at the pick-up point. I just ran a mile with a German Shepherd chasing me while I was carrying all of my gear," he yelled.

I yelled back, "You're wearing a camouflage shirt and pants standing amongst the trees. I am surprised the dog even saw you."

"Take me to the hospital," he said.

"Did the dog bite you?" I asked worriedly.

"No, I can hardly see," he responded.

His eyes were almost swollen shut, so I drove an hour to the only hospital. When we got there, it was completely quiet. We stood there confused. Suddenly, a very excited new doctor greeted us. He at once got to work on Scott, who was probably the only patient he had seen in weeks judging by the empty parking lot and shiniest floors I had ever seen.

The doctor asked Scott questions as he examined him and helped him slowly unravel the mystery as he traced his steps from the day before.

The doctor determined that Scott had fertilizer on his hands and rubbed his eyes absent-mindedly before washing his hands.

The good news was that his vision would be fine. The bad news was that the doctor had to put some medicated gel into Scott's eyes that instantly turned the whites of his eyes bright yellow like French's mustard. With his whole face swollen and his eyes so yellow, he was so unrecognizable that I could have passed him on the street dressed in camouflage or not.

We left the hospital, and it started to pour again. We were hungry and decided to get something to eat. Scott could not be in public. Being 6 feet, 4 inches tall with glowing yellow eyes and dressed in camouflage from head to toe made him quite terrifying, like a monster from a low-budget horror movie.

We went back to the restaurant across the street from our hotel and ordered takeout again. We brought it back to our dark, windowless dungeon-like hotel and ate. The food was still just OK. It rained harder and harder. There was nothing, and I mean nothing, on TV. We went to sleep early.

The next day it continued to pour. Scott was still not human enough looking to reemerge into the real world yet. There was still nothing on TV, and we got more food which was just OK. We were so bored.

We drove home the next day, wondering why we even bothered. We agreed that it was the worst getaway. And we were never going back to that OK restaurant rain or shine, with eyes swollen shut or open, or to that windowless dungeon of a hotel room.

Life Lesson: Keep your fingers out of your eyes, and don't wear camouflage when waiting for someone to pick you up on the side of a country road.

THAT'S UNFORTUNATE

Chapter Twenty

AGING GRACEFULLY

When Scott's hair started turning grey in his twenties, I suggested that we dye it. I saw a commercial for Just For Men hair dye and was impressed by its ease of use and its natural appearance on the actor. What could possibly go wrong?

I went to CVS and found Scott's shade, dark brown. I waited for him to come home from work and showed him the box when he walked through the door.

"This is going to be so easy," I enthusiastically told him.

Scott had no interest in dying his hair, but he agreed to do it since it was so simple, and I was so excited about it. We went over the instructions together.

"You just lather the dye into your hair, and when it's time, you just rinse it out," I explained.

He was surprisingly patient after a long day at work. "I sleep with this in my hair?" he asked.

I laughed, "No, that would be so messy! You rinse it out after ten minutes."

I was secretly jealous at the ease of using Just For Men and contemplated getting it in Auburn for myself. My hair dye had to be precisely applied with a brush and left on my hair for an hour.

Scott went into the bathroom and applied his hair dye. After ten minutes, he hopped into the shower and emerged as a brunette, once again looking not a day over twenty-five.

"You look fantastic!" I told him.

He was indifferent but pleased that I liked it.

When Scott's grey started coming through again, I went back to CVS. This time, they did not have the dark brown dye. I assumed it was the most popular shade, and with Thanksgiving in four days, the gentlemen probably wanted to look their best.

I should have gone to another store, but I didn't. In cooking, I am the queen of substitution, and it was no different in hair dye. I studied the available colors and chuckled at the thought of making Scott a ginger as I held the red box of dye. I decided to go with the color jet black. His hair was very dark brown. What is the difference, right?

Again, I gave the box of hair dye to Scott when he came through the door after work.

He looked at the package and said," It's jet black!"

I assured him it would be fine and sent him to the bathroom for application. When Scott emerged from the bathroom after rinsing out the black hair dye, I was shocked. It really was jet black. I hoped his hair was still wet and that it would dry to his natural dark brown color or at least close to it. Nope, when it dried, it was somehow darker. Neither of us said anything about it. I figured that since Scott didn't seem to notice that maybe no one else would. Over the next couple of days, I got used to it, sort of, I guess.

On Thanksgiving, we went to Scott's parent's house. His two brothers were already there with their wives when we arrived.

The first thing his mother said when she saw Scott was, "You look so pale!"

I immediately became defensive and said, "He is fine!"

Scott and I had only been married for three years, and as a newer bride, I felt the self-imposed pressure to prove that I could take care of my mother-in-law's son perfectly well. She was right, though. He did look quite pale. But I knew that I was feeding him and taking good care of him, and he only looked pale because his hair was now jet black. They would get used to it, I assured myself.

Dinner was delicious, and the conversation and laughter flowed easily. Then the comments about Scott's hair started again, and I could feel my guard go up.

"You're so thin and pale!" his mother exclaimed, looking at Scott.

Of course, his father chimed in, "Is Kim feeding you enough?"

Everyone laughed, except me. I was becoming increasingly more furious by the second. Yes, Scott had lost weight, but it was because of his ass problems from bouncing around in his dump truck and backhoe every day. He was eating lighter and adding more fiber to his diet until the ass situation calmed down, as per the doctor's orders.

Then our sister-in-law Barbara said, "Yeah, your chest looks concave. How much weight have you lost?"

I was fuming. I loved Scott's family, but my goodness, they could latch onto a topic like a dog with a bone and refuse to let it go. The rest of the night continued with remarks here and there about Scott's suddenly too fair complexion, weight loss, and jokes about me starving him.

I should have just confessed that I made him accidentally dye his hair jet black. Everyone would have thought it was hysterical, and the concern for Scott's health would have been put to rest. But I was too embarrassed, and quite frankly, my blood was boiling at that point.

When we got into the car, Scott said, “I knew my hair was too dark. I look ridiculous.”

He was right. We drove home in silence.

I never bought another box of Just For Men hair dye in dark brown or any other color. I just let Scott age gracefully. It was easier that way.

Life Lesson: If you don’t see your right hair dye color, go to another store. It is worth the extra effort every time.

Chapter Twenty-One

NO PICKLES OR OLIVES, PLEASE!

A month before I got married, there was so much happening. My parents were in the middle of putting put an addition on our house and were busy preparing for my wedding, while they each worked sixty hours a week.

One morning, I went to the kitchen to have something to eat. I opened the fridge, and it was practically empty except for condiments and a couple of jars of dill pickles and Greek olives. While I loved those things, I certainly could not make a substantial meal from them.

My bed frame had also broken on the left bottom corner the day before, causing the whole bed to slump down sharply to one side, rendering it useless.

Immediately, the commercials for *Save The Children* popped into my head.

I smiled, knowing exactly how to resolve the situation.

I left a note on the fridge describing my current plight. Tell me if this sounds familiar.

Kimberly is twenty-two years old and lives in Northern New Jersey. She eats only dill pickles and Greek olives and at night goes to sleep in her broken bed.

There are children all over the world living under these conditions. You can't help all of them, but you can help Kimberly.

You will experience the joy of giving as you see Kimberly's progress each week through letters and pictures.

Please send non-perishable food and a new bed frame quickly so Kimberly can have a decent meal and a restful night's sleep.

P.S. Please do not send any pickles or olives.

It worked!

Hours later, the fridge was full! We had a satisfying dinner of stuffed pork loin, grilled asparagus, and baked potatoes. My new bed frame arrived the next day. I was well-fed, well-rested, and all was good.

Life Lesson: Never underestimate the power of laughter, a hearty meal, a good night's sleep, and a little guilt.

Chapter Twenty-Two

IMPOSTERS

Our family was in Lancaster for the day and stopped at the best buffet around. It was 10:30 AM and still breakfast time. Lunch started at 11:00. Scott wondered if we should wait until 11:00 for lunch.

"Amateur," I thought.

We hadn't eaten anything yet and were famished. I devised a foolproof plan.

"We go in for breakfast, have some coffee, a pancake, a little bacon, and then wait for lunch," I said.

The lunch menu was much better since there was steak, shrimp, chicken wings, dumplings, gravy, and more, not to mention the Pennsylvania Dutch favorites like shoofly pie and way too much sauerkraut.

My plan worked. We took it easy for breakfast and just nibbled so we could save ourselves for the better fare at lunch. Once 11 AM came, the four of us scattered in all directions. The buffet was huge. Scott headed towards the meat and potatoes, Veronica towards the fried stuff, Victoria the seafood area, and I went towards the salad bar.

I made a beautiful salad with mixed greens, grilled chicken, bacon, red onions, carrots, hot peppers, feta cheese and topped my creation with a creamy peppercorn dressing. The only thing that was missing was olives. Then, I spotted a massive bowl of the most stunning black olives I had ever seen. They were the size of globe grapes and were so shiny and firm looking. I reached for the serving spoon and, upon closer inspection, realized that they were ultra-dark chocolate-covered raisin clusters. While I didn't want the chocolate-covered raisins in my salad, I put some into a small side dish for our table to enjoy. Still perplexed at why this bowl of confections was placed at the salad bar and not the dessert area, I was distracted by some pickled beets and walked to the other side of the salad bar.

Before I could warn her, a woman walked up excitedly to the tempting bowl of imposter olives and put two big scoops on her salad. Then I watched in horror as she topped it with extra chunky blue dressing. There was no point in saying anything since she looked so happy, for now anyway.

I looked around for my husband and girls to share this story. I couldn't find them. The woman started walking away, so I followed her to her table. I needed to know what happened next. Fortunately for me, her table was by the self-serve drink station. I pretended to fill my glass with seltzer while I peered at her through a potted plant, waiting for her reaction.

She was talking to her husband while she picked up her fork.

"Hurry up already!" I whispered encouragingly.

She took a bite and seemed quite pleased.

A sly smile crept across my face as I thought, "The next bite is going to be a shock."

She pierced what she thought was an olive with her fork and dipped it into the thick blue cheese dressing. She put it into her mouth and chewed. Her eyes suddenly became giant as a look of confusion mixed with disgust washed over her face. She quickly grabbed her napkin and spat out the offending item. Then she inspected it and showed it to her husband. He took one of the so-called olives from her plate that was not covered in dressing and ate it. He started laughing and told her it was a dark chocolate-covered raisin.

"Why did you put that on your salad?" he asked.

"I thought they were olives. They were in a bowl on the salad bar next to the salad dressing," she said defensively.

"It may not be an olive, but that is the best chocolate-covered raisin I ever had. Go back and get more, only no blue cheese this time," he teased.

She pushed her plate aside, laughed, and went back to the buffet, certain, I'm sure, not to make that mistake again.

I thought about telling our server to move the chocolate-covered raisins to the dessert area or at least put a sign next to them indicating they were raisins. Nah, they were perfect where they were just waiting for an unsuspecting olive lover to come along and make a truly unforgettable salad.

Life Lesson: I hate admitting it but, chocolate does not go with everything.

Chapter Twenty-Three

I'D LIKE TO SLAP YOU

It had been snowing for four days in a row. Scott was exhausted from plowing. The girls and I took turns keeping him company and shoveling walkways to save his back.

In between snowstorms, I had to get my daughter ready to go to an event in Atlantic City. She was a NJ state delegate for DECA, which is a high school debate competition. The stakes were high, with thousands of students from our state competing to make it to the final round in Orlando and be crowned the DECA grand champion.

We shopped for business wear, shoes, and snacks for Victoria. It took five stores, but we did it! Then, I was asked to be one of the judges at the last minute, and I had to run back to the stores for myself.

The big day was here. I helped Victoria pack, and I dropped her off at school bright and early. The bus was waiting to take the entire DECA entourage, which included the student delegates, teachers, chaperones, and even a security guard with a stun gun. You never know when a stun gun will come in handy, especially in Atlantic City. It gets wild there!

I had to drive my car, which is best since I get terrible motion sickness on buses. Since I would be passing my parent's house, I stopped on the way and had a wonderful dinner with my mom and dad, and continued the drive to Atlantic City.

It was getting late, and I was tired from not only the long drive but the lack of sleep from all-night snow shoveling, marathon shopping sprees, and frantic packing. I finally made it to Atlantic City. I got lost even with GPS due to the one-way streets. I saw the sign for the Hard Rock Hotel, and let out a sigh of relief. I pulled into the parking garage like I was instructed to do and parked on level 1J.

I grabbed my admittedly over-packed suitcases and headed to the elevators. Upon exiting the elevator, I was immediately confronted with a situation. The way onto the main floor of the hotel was down a two-story super skinny escalator. With my fear of heights and my wide suitcases, I envisioned myself getting dizzy and toppling all the way down the escalator. That was not the entrance I wanted to make into the lobby, especially being a DECA judge.

So, I dragged my luggage down two flights of stairs, feeling proud that I had averted an embarrassing fall. As I walked, I started to sweat. It had to be at least 80 degrees, almost as hot as my in-law's house, almost.

I kept looking for an elevator down to the next level where the reservation desk was. There was none—just a three-story escalator which seemed even more narrow than the previous one. I thought, who the hell designed this hotel? I internally screamed curse words that would make a truck driver blush. I was so bone-weary, sweaty, hungry, and extremely frustrated at this point.

I found a security guard who kindly offered to watch my luggage while I went downstairs to check in. I was pleased because I was finally making progress.

There was no line, and I got help right away. My momentary joy quickly extinguished when the young woman behind the desk politely informed me that there was no reservation under my name, and she had never heard of DECA. I think I blacked out for a moment from the shock.

I could hear my daughter's words echoing in my head, "Yeah, it's at the Hard Rock Hotel."

Dammit, I fell for it again. Victoria has a way of saying things in such a matter-of-fact way that you just don't doubt her.

It made me question her career path as a nurse, and I envisioned her telling the doctor, "Yes, the patient is definitely O negative."

I rolled my eyes in annoyance. I never hit my children, but for a split second wanted to slap Victoria. My judging invitation was last minute. Victoria filled out my paperwork, so I never saw the hotel's name in writing.

I called Victoria, and she told me, "Your reservation is at Harrah's.

"What?" I yelled. "You told me it was the Hard Rock Hotel!"

"Oh, sorry," she said, not realizing what I was currently going through.

I had a mini freak out at the reservation counter. The young woman said that she understood how upset I was. But I could tell she was wondering if she should call security.

"A wild redhead is screaming about something called DECA and saying that she wants to slap someone named Victoria. Bring your stun gun," I imagined her saying.

I took the walk of shame and rage, back to the security guard, and retrieved my cumbersome luggage. I never traveled alone. Scott always carried my luggage, so I did not realize that although the suitcases had two wheels, they were still heavy and awkward.

I managed to get onto the impossibly narrow escalator with my suitcases. As I was nearing the top, I knew I had to be ready to get off quickly. I tried to maneuver my luggage for a graceful exit, but one of the suitcases became wedged at the top of the escalator, making me fall over it and onto the landing. I got up and yanked my suitcase as hard as I could to release it. I wiped the sweat from my brow and wondered how much more I could take?

I made it to the elevator, and I pushed level 1. I welcomed the cold crisp air after escaping the sauna-like conditions in the casino. The doors opened, and I saw level 1E.

No big deal, right? 1J must be close. As I walked and walked up the incline in the parking garage, my damn suitcases felt heavier and heavier. My shoulders were burning, my back ached, and my new shoes were so uncomfortable. I breathlessly looked up, and I was only on level 1F. An unladylike tirade of curse words I didn't even realize I knew erupted from my lips.

I saw my solution, a stairwell.

My mother's words rang through my head, "Be careful in the parking garage in Atlantic City and stay out of the stairwells. They are dangerous."

I pressed on and dragged those suitcases up two flights of stairs. Honestly, I would have welcomed death at this point. But I felt confident that the anger coursing through my veins was enough to fuel me in fighting off anyone foolishly waiting in the stairwell to attack me. They didn't stand a chance. I was on a rampage.

I victoriously emerged from the stairwell alive and with my luggage. And then I saw it. Level 2E. At this point, I yelled in frustration.

I heard my words, "Why me?" echo through the vacant parking garage.

I sat down on my suitcase and wept. I thought about opening my bags and taking my laptop and my new curling wand, and abandoning the rest of it, especially the painful shoes I was wearing.

I pulled myself together and headed back into the inferno-like casino. I shoved my luggage onto the stupid skinny escalator and took it up to the same elevator I took to enter this Godforsaken place an hour ago.

At this point, I was a broken woman. I had no confidence that I would ever make it back to my car. I said a prayer for mercy. The elevator door opened. I swear I heard angels sing. A bright light shone on the wall and illuminated the letters '1J.' Was it a mirage? No, the Mirage Casino was in Vegas. I was trapped in the Hard Rock Hotel in Atlantic City.

Now, I could see my car from the elevator. When I made it to my car, I contemplated driving the three hours home. But I made a commitment to my daughter and DECA. Drenched in sweat, I turned on the air conditioning even though it was 40 degrees outside. The cool air revived me. I popped a handful of Valerian root capsules and doused myself in lavender essential oil to settle my nerves. After all, I had to prepare to do this all over again at Harrah's.

I arrived at Harrah's and took a deep breath as I entered the parking garage. I dragged my luggage out of the trunk and walked to the elevator. Upon entering the hotel, I found myself confronted with the same two-story super skinny escalator nonsense. Was this a cruel, twisted joke?

I saw a security guard by the escalator. He greeted me kindly.

"You have no idea what I have been through," I said.

Tears welled up in my eyes. I was so disheveled at this point and was limping from my painfully tight but stunning new shoes.

The nice man took pity on me and brought my suitcases down the escalator. Now, safely on the ground floor, I headed towards the reservation desk. After a mile or so of weaving through the casino full of drunk people, I made it. There were only seven people ahead of me to check into the hotel. The line should move quickly, I thought.

Wrong! I waited for an hour in line. It was now 10 PM, but at least I had my room key. The hotel was bustling, and there was no bellhop to bring my luggage to my room. I couldn't wait any longer. I dragged my luggage to the elevator but was devastated to see a long line.

At 10:23 PM, I made it to my room. It was beautiful and very well deserved. I put down the luggage I had come to resent, kicked off my shoes, and called room service for a glass of wine.

"Sorry, room service ended at 10 PM. You can go down to the bar in the lobby," he said, trying to be helpful.

I said something snarky, hung up the phone and felt no guilt after what I experienced. I got changed, crawled into bed, and was so happy to relax finally. A tear of joy rolled down my cheek, and I quickly fell asleep.

The following day, I had breakfast with the other judges, and we received instruction on the judging criteria. When it was time to begin, I could see Victoria from across the room looking confident and poised as she gave her presentation to one of the judges. I was so impressed by these young adults and proud of every one of them, especially my daughter. They were all extraordinary.

Later that day, I checked out of the hotel and took the trek back to my car, dragging my luggage through the casino. The security guard recognized me and brought my bags up the escalator, and put them in the elevator for me.

"Bless you," I said.

I drove to my parent's house an hour away. We had a lovely meal of chicken Milanese, a mixed greens salad, and red wine. I told my harrowing story, and we all laughed, although my mother was upset that I was walking around in the empty parking garages and stairwells.

My mom and I played Upwords until I became too tired and needed to go to bed. I walked upstairs to my room and realized that I had left my suitcase downstairs. I couldn't pick that hateful thing up again and was too exhausted to go up and down any more stairs. I slept in my clothes and did not care.

When I got home the next day, I emptied my suitcases and threw them right into the garbage. I thought about riding over them with my car but was tired of driving, even if it was only back and forth in my driveway, crushing the worst luggage ever. No wonder my mother got new luggage and passed it on to me. Maybe I should have slapped both my mother and Victoria?

. . .

Life Lesson: Purchase light luggage with four wheels and always confirm your travel plans, so you don't have the urge to slap everyone.

Chapter Twenty-Four

HONK, HONK GOES 'THE GOOSE MAN'

Anyone who has been in a relationship for a long time knows that it's the little things that your partner does that drive you nuts. I've been married to Scott for thirty years. There is an extensive list, but what aggravates me the most is his selective sense of smell, penchant for destroying things without realizing it and blaming someone else, and starting unnecessary projects at the most inopportune time. But by far, the worst is the annoying noises he makes due to his allergies.

Scott often becomes offended by innocuous smells.

Sometimes, he'll say, "What's gone bad in the refrigerator?"

After an exhaustive search, he finds the culprit; a single cherry that has dried up in the back of the fridge.

"Yes, that was it!" he'll say with certainty.

But when it's hazardous, he can't smell it.

Numerous times, I have asked Scott, "Do you smell gas?"

He never does. Meanwhile, I'll suddenly notice that he did not completely turn off the gas burner knob on the stove, allowing gas to leak.

Scott is also handy; he can fix pretty much anything. However, this also leads to destruction. and he always responds with, "That wasn't me." He believes it, too, but of course, I have learned through experience that it's always him.

Years ago, I upgraded our internet, phone, and television service, and a technician came to our house. He was a very nice young man. He didn't need to go inside, and only a few connections outside had to be adjusted. I saw him sit down at my new wooden patio table and tighten the screws on a part he had to install for the new service. Then he got out a small hammer and started tapping on it. After a bit, he got up from the table, installed the new parts, and was on his way.

The next day, I was furious to see that my new wooden table had seven large deep indentations spanning a two-foot area across the tabletop exactly where the technician was sitting the day before. When Scott got home, I showed it to him.

He instantly said, "That wasn't me. It had to be the cable guy yesterday."

I called the cable company in hopes they would replace my table, and an investigator came out that day. She was a tough cookie and very thorough. After conducting her investigation, she determined that her technician was not responsible for the damage.

"The indentations on the tabletop are from a screw head that is different from the equipment that he installed here," she happily informed me.

I disagreed, "I saw him sitting here working at the table, and the next day, I saw the indentations on my tabletop."

"Impossible, case closed," she said. "Maybe it was your husband?"

I was so annoyed; how dare she blame Scott when I saw the technician ruin the table? When Scott came home, I told him what had happened. We went over to the table, and he looked closer and thought for a moment.

"You know what, I think it was me. I was fixing the hedge trimmer on the table. Sorry."

"OMG, are you kidding me? I should have known it was you," I yelled.

Scott also enjoys starting unimportant projects moments before leaving for vacation or before guests are about to arrive. One year we were hosting Thanksgiving, Scott decided that this was the perfect time to pull everything out of the mudroom closet and replace a broken floor tile way in the back. He was still cleaning up when the guests arrived.

The thing that gets under my skin the most is his daily nose-blowing due to his seasonal allergies, which is a problem for him during every friggin' season. It's like living with a goose. He's honking when he first wakes up, during the day, and right before bed. The sound of him clearing his nasal passages with such force is like nails on a chalkboard to me. I am instantly unnerved when I hear it, and the only thing that settles me down is imagining hitting him over the head with a 2 x 4.

Although she has not endured the incessant honking for as long as I have, my daughter, Veronica, completely understands how I feel. Whenever we hear it, we look at each other as I mimic clunking Scott over the head, and we laugh, which thankfully diffuses our irritation.

Because of him, the sound of geese honking in the wild sets me off and makes me want to clunk him over the head even if he is nowhere in sight.

Scott has earned a slew of nicknames through the years, one of the most fitting being 'The Goose Man.'

Life Lesson: Love is blind, not deaf. Honk, honk!

Chapter Twenty-Five

THAT REALLY STINKS!

When Scott returned from a successful salmon fishing trip in Alaska, he received the unfortunate news that the airline had lost his 100 lbs. of frozen fish.

“Don’t worry, we will find it!” the woman on the phone assured him.

Hours passed, and there was still no word. Scott called again, getting worried that his fish would spoil if not found soon. He was connected with a supervisor from FEDEX who promised that it would be delivered by morning. Scott said to leave the fish in the freezer located in the garage.

We heard the garage door open at 5 AM. When Scott went downstairs in the morning, he was relieved to see his salmon in the freezer. We moved the fish into the freezer in the basement.

Six months later, I went to the basement to vacuum, but no empty outlets were available on that side of the room. I decided to unplug the freezer so I could use the vacuum. When finished, I went back upstairs.

A couple of weeks went by, and Scott noticed that the tiny orange freezer light on the front of the lid was not on.

"Oh no, please no!" he said.

Scott opened the top of the freezer and was hit by the stench of rotten fish. He called me down. He was mad and revolted, mostly revolted.

The freezer had defrosted entirely. If we could have carried the whole freezer up the stairs and outside, we would have. There was only one thing to do; get plastic bags and clean the freezer out.

It was the worst thing I had ever smelled. I held the garbage bag and my nose while Scott reached into the deep freeze and pulled out bag after bag of dripping rotten fish. He kept gagging, so he tied a red bandana over his nose and mouth and went back into the freezer headfirst.

After a few more minutes, I couldn't take it anymore and dashed outside for some fresh air. I peered into the basement window and watched Scott. We had made more progress than I thought. He put the remaining fish into a garbage bag and then started wiping the bottom of the freezer with a towel. As he pulled the towel out to put it in the garbage bag, I saw the slime that covered the towel stretch like a rubber band, and I dry-heaved as it snapped back into the freezer. Scott gagged also. Feeling guilty for abandoning him in his time of need, I went back inside to help.

It was still disgusting even with the spoiled fish removed. Now it wasn't so much the stench but the texture of the slippery stringy slime that was revolting. Every time Scott gagged, I gagged from hearing him gag and vice versa. It was a vicious cycle of dry heaving.

When the dry heaving stopped and the air smelled good again, we wanted to laugh, but it was still too soon. It was also too soon to eat any fish, especially salmon.

Life Lesson: Don't touch the plug to the freezer, ever.

IT JUST DOESN'T FIT

Chapter Twenty-Six

YOU WON'T LIKE ME WHEN I AM ANGRY

I was invited to a casual springtime party and wanted a new outfit. I found a beautiful pair of linen-like pants and a short, fitted jacket with large square brass buttons. There was only one outfit in this style left at the store. Although it was a size or two larger than I usually wear, I bought the outfit anyway, intending to alter it. I loved it!

When I met with the tailor, she asked me to try both pieces on. We decided that I needed the hem shortened and the legs narrowed on the pants. The waist needed to be taken in on both the pants and the jacket. She agreed it was an adorable outfit.

The tailor asked to take a quick peek at the label to see what material the manufacturer used to make the outfit. After noting the fabric, she recommended that I wash the clothing first since there may be slight shrinkage from laundering. Then, I should return for alterations, if needed.

When I got home, I went directly to the laundry room. I looked at the care tags on both garments and followed the instructions exactly: cold water, delicate cycle, dryer on low heat. Easy enough, right?

When the washing cycle finished, I removed the pants and jacket from the machine and inspected them. To my disappointment, they both seemed to be the same size still. I was hoping to avoid the hassle of going back to the tailor for alterations. I put the outfit into the dryer on low heat with high hopes that it would fit just right after drying.

As I was making dinner, the dryer buzzed to alert me that the cycle had completed. I rushed to grab my hopefully perfectly fitting outfit and went upstairs to try it on with my new navy heels.

I put on the pants, jacket, and shoes and looked at myself in the mirror. I laughed out loud. Before washing, the pants were three inches too long, the legs were much too wide, and the waist was about two inches too big. The jacket just needed to be taken in at the waist.

Now, here I stood in knee-length pants that were so skin-tight that I could not zip them. The jacket had shrunken so much that I could not lift my arms. The buttons were so strained they looked like they were going to pop and injure someone.

I was reminded of Dr. David Banner's warning before something enraged him, and he morphed into The Incredible Hulk as his clothing became tighter and tighter.

"Don't make me angry. You won't like me when I am angry."

I was going for an easy, breezy look. Instead, I was bursting out of my suddenly tiny outfit, looking like a much paler but well-put-together version of the Incredible Hulk. As I laughed, I thought about how furious I would have been if I had this outfit altered before I washed it.

Life Lesson: Don't get angry, even when your clothes don't fit. It may make it worse.

Chapter Twenty-Seven

WHAT THE HELL HAPPENED?

Before Scott and I got married, we took the ten-hour drive to North Carolina to pick out new furniture. Five hours in the car is my limit. Driving long distances with me is like traveling with a puppy. I get car sick, I must urinate frequently, I need snacks, and the window needs to be rolled down in case I need to vomit from the nauseating motion of the car. Fortunately, I also pass out for long stretches and miss seeing entire states, which helps Scott make up for lost time driving.

We had a wonderful time picking out just the right pieces for our home. The stores were nice enough to coordinate so everything could ship together on one truck.

When we were in the last store, I saw a gorgeous painting to put over the sofa. It was in the impressionistic style and featured a pond with a winding path through frosty pine trees. The sky depicted a perfect sunset in soft pink, peach, and yellow and was reflected in the clear blue water. I was mesmerized and looked at it longingly, knowing the painting would match the cushions I selected for the couch perfectly. Yet, I said nothing since Scott had already bought so much furniture.

As we made our way home, I couldn't stop thinking about the painting. I told Scott how much I loved it, and since we were only twenty minutes into the trip, he turned around and drove back for the painting.

I ran into the store and asked the salesperson to add the artwork to our furniture shipment. He told me that he could not add the painting to the load, and I would have to take it with me.

I went out to the car to give Scott the news. He was already irritated but got out of the car and started to adjust the front seats and items in the back seat. I went back into the store for painting. The salesperson wrapped it up for me but had to take a phone call. I didn't want to wait, so I decided to take the painting to the car myself. It was so big that I had trouble stretching my arms enough to carry it. I finally got a good enough grip on it and headed outside.

Once I made it outdoors, a powerful gust of wind came and almost knocked me down as I struggled to walk with my new masterpiece. There was not a tree in sight to block the wind, just an open space, and the big wind gusts made it so hard to walk with this enormous painting. I finally made it to the car, parked at the furthest possible point in the lot, which Scott loves to do.

I was shocked when I saw Scott.

"I was gone for ten minutes! What the hell happened?" I asked.

Scott was standing there covered in blood. It was on his face, shirt, hands, pants, and all over the car. A quarter got stuck in the track under the driver's seat while Scott tried to make room for the painting. He cut himself up trying to get the quarter out. We were not in his truck, so Scott didn't have any tools. He was furious at this point. Scott grabbed the painting from me and managed to get it into the backseat after tricky maneuvering and swearing.

But now we had another issue. The painting was so big that the only way it would fit was to move our seats up to the closet position and tilt them forward. I looked over at Scott as he started to drive towards the exit of the parking lot. His chest was practically touching the steering wheel. Our heads were inches from the windshield. The thought of sitting in this uncomfortable position for ten hours was unbearable. I demanded that he stop the car.

We got out of the car, and he roughly pulled the painting out of the backseat. I got it out of his hands before he snapped it in half. As I was trying to wrap my arms around this giant painting, the wind kicked up again. At least this time, the wind was at my back, and it blew me and the picture right into the store almost effortlessly. Scott later told me it was like watching a sailboat when the wind catches the sails.

I described the bloodbath situation in my car to the shocked salesperson. With my Jersey Girl attitude in full force, I firmly told him to do whatever it took to get the painting on the truck with the rest of the furniture. I refused to take no for an answer. After an intense conversation with the shipping department, the salesperson was successful!

I got back into the car, and Scott and I drove in silence. I didn't care since I was just grateful that we were sitting upright without our heads pressed up against the windshield. Thirty minutes later, Scott admitted that he felt guilty for making me struggle with that painting through the windy parking lot twice. He apologized.

For years we when we looked at the beautiful painting hanging over our couch, we laughed, remembering the ferocious wind, the splattered blood, and the fun we had driving home.

Life Lesson: If it's not a good fit, don't force it.

Chapter Twenty-Eight

DÉJÀ VU

After giving birth to my first daughter, a nurse brought me to my hospital room at 4 AM. She told me that my roommate had a son a couple of days earlier and was leaving that morning, and I would have the room to myself. I was grateful because I had been up for twenty-four hours at that point and was exhausted.

The new mom and dad were nervous about leaving with their baby and kept stalling. They changed the baby's outfit four times because nothing fit him since he was only five pounds. Then the new mom decided to take a shower. Then the couple tried to buckle the baby into his car seat, and they couldn't get the straps tight enough. Then her lunch came. Now the baby's diaper had to be changed, and that meant another wardrobe change. Then she wanted to feed him one more time.

I was screaming on the inside, "Just go!"

There was so much commotion, and I just wanted them to leave. Finally, I was alone and able to rest for a bit.

When it was my turn to go home with my daughter, I was terrified. Scott showed up and helped me pack my things. I felt guilty about the thoughts I had about my roommate a couple of days earlier. Now I understood how she felt. I didn't want to leave either. I didn't know what to do with my baby, who was tiny and screamed a lot.

The nurse came in and showed us how to buckle little Victoria into her car seat. She helped me into the wheelchair with the enormous car seat containing the screaming baby placed in my lap.

I asked, "You're going to let us leave with her? I don't know what I am doing."

The nurse assured me that we would do just fine. I wasn't so sure, but I appreciated the confidence she had in my mothering skills even though I had never changed a diaper before.

Scott pulled my small Volvo S40 up to the curb. The nurse helped buckle the baby seat into the car and reminded us that the baby seat had to be backward facing. The car seat was quite large, and I bought my car before I was pregnant, so it was not exactly a roomy mom car. We had to push the seats up as far as possible to accommodate the colossal car seat.

The nurse waved goodbye and said, "Good luck!"

We were going to need it. Scott and I got into the car. I was cramped at 5' 4" but was way more comfortable than my 6' 4" tall husband. His knees were touching the steering wheel. Both of our seats were leaning forward so much that our heads were almost touching the windshield.

Scott's tension was palpable. He didn't say anything right away, but I knew he was annoyed. Before we made it out of the parking lot, he said what was on his mind.

"We just got the baby, and already the new car is useless," he said with disbelief.

It reminded me of the trip home from North Carolina when Scott was covered with blood from trying to fit a massive painting in the back of our car. That was the first time we had to push our seats up and angle them so far forward that our heads were touching the windshield. This ride was déjà vu at its worst; only there was not any blood this time. At least in North Carolina, I convinced the store manager to ship the painting to us, but I couldn't ship the baby home. Thank God, it was only a ten-minute ride.

We drove home in silence, except for the crying; Scott because the car was too small, me because I was afraid of the baby, and the baby because she probably sensed that her parents had no idea what they were doing.

I was able to find a smaller car seat so we could sit comfortably in the car, and there was less crying all around, especially from Scott. I was still a little afraid of the baby, though.

Life Lesson: Don't buy a baby seat bigger than the backseat of your car.

Chapter Twenty-Nine

GENERATED DRAMA

I love a good storm. To me, there is nothing more snuggly than being tucked safely inside of the house with a roaring fire, a pot of stew on the stove, cookies in the oven, and playing games with the family while all hell breaks loose outside.

One of the worst storms I have ever experienced in our area was Superstorm Sandy. The weather channels salivate over big storms with the possibility of destruction and seem to enjoy instilling the panic-filled dashes to the store for eggs, bread, milk, and wine, don't forget the wine.

I took this storm warning very seriously. It would be a doozy and would cause massive destruction from wind, and coastal storm surges were expected to cause severe flooding even in areas that didn't typically flood. Everyone was warned to prepare for power outages, have a month's food and drinking water supply, fill up your gas tanks, and have twenty extra gallons of gas on hand. Purchasing a generator was also recommended.

I sprang into action, and the first thing I did was order a generator. I found one online for $350, which was fortunate because a few days later, the price for the same generator jumped to $1000, and by the following week, no generators were available anywhere to purchase.

Scott filled the vehicles with gas and had thirty gallons in gas cans behind the shed.

Meanwhile, I collected a month's supply of food and water. We were ready to face this thing head-on.

We watched the storm come up the coast and were shocked by the devastation it caused to anything in its path. We saw footage of high-force winds knocking down trees and crushing houses while other houses were submerged by water. Many people did not heed the evacuation warnings and were trapped since it was too dangerous to rescue them due to the storm surges.

I started to feel concerned. When the first gust of wind came, knocking down several trees in the woods behind our house, I braced for the worst.

The storm passed, and to my surprise, not much had happened around our house. We never lost power, no more trees fell, and there was no water damage. Oddly, I was a little disappointed since I was uber prepared. My mom, unfortunately, lost power and was not as prepared. I offered her my generator, and she accepted.

A few days later, our power went out. Apparently, at the bottom of our hill, a tree was leaning on the power lines. The power was disconnected so the tree could be cut. We expected another crew to arrive within the hour to reconnect the power. They never came since there were thousands of trees down and many roads were impassable. Crews from all over the country arrived to help with the disaster.

The next day our power was still out. Around 5 PM, I called my mom and asked her if she could borrow a generator from someone and return mine. Luckily, her boss in Connecticut had one she could borrow. She returned my generator and drove with my father to meet her boss a couple of hours away. It took so long with so many trees down and flooding.

That night, Scott and I took the girls to the diner for dinner to celebrate the return of our generator. Halfway through our meal, the phone rings, it was my mother. My heart sank, "Now what?" I wondered. I could not take any more generator drama.

Scott asked, "Don't tell me that the generator doesn't fit into their car?"

I laughed and said, "Close, it's the wrong kind of plug. It won't fit into their panel." She took the generator anyway and is going to drive back to our house and see if it will plug into our panel."

In the morning, we woke up and saw that our generator was gone and replaced with the generator from Connecticut. Thankfully, the plug fit into our panel, and the 'generated drama' was over, at last.

Life Lesson: Sometimes, the weather channel gets it right.

FUNNY CHURCH STUFF

Chapter Thirty

THAT'S THE LIMO?

I sat in disbelief in the back of a cargo van. The day's events flashed in my mind.

It had been a perfect day in late June. The sun was bright, the sky was clear, and the air was warm with a soft breeze. It was my wedding day! I married a wonderful man, and all the people I loved most were there to help us celebrate.

The food was delectable, the music was fantastic, and the joy from dancing, love, laughter, and blessings from all in attendance filled the room. Every detail was painstakingly elegant, right down to the ice sculptures, white-glove service, and the elaborate cake with multiple bridges leading to more tiers of the cake. If you knew my mother, you would understand.

Scott and I said our goodbyes to our guests and thanked everyone, especially our parents, for making this a magical day.

My Aunt Gayle gave me one last hug before I left. She told me how spectacular the day was, how beautiful I looked and how thrilled she was for me.

As she straightened my pearl and sapphire necklace, she said, "It is a shame about your last name, though."

I burst out laughing. Gayle was right. My maiden name was melodious and lovely, unlike this short, flat, guttural sounding last name I now claimed as my own.

I felt like a princess. I waved and blew kisses as we made our grand exit. Our parents followed us outside and wished us all the best before we left to start our new lives together. As we were saying our goodbyes, we were interrupted by our limo driver, who informed us that it was time to go.

I turned around and was baffled. "Where is the limo?" I asked.

"Right here!" the driver impatiently responded as he guided us towards a van that had 'The Ramada Inn' written across the door.

Before I could respond, the driver gently shoved me into the back of the van. I was too shocked to react. The only missing thing was duct tape over my mouth and rope to bind my hands behind my back.

I looked at my husband and said, "What happened to the limo the venue promised us?

Our gazes met briefly with the newly married and equally confused couple huddled in the back of the van between stacks of fresh linens and boxes of stemware.

Dazed, we waved to our proud parents as we were whisked away in what felt like a kidnapping.

I sat motionless in my poufy wedding dress and tiara. I looked forward, avoiding eye contact with the other couple and anyone on the highway who may have been looking on, wondering, "What the hell am I witnessing?" I imagined my arch-nemesis from high school driving by pointing, laughing, and feeling superior at last.

We pulled into the hotel parking lot, and all quickly exited the van in silence, inwardly vowing to never speak of this. However, I had to break my silence, so this never happens to anyone ever again.

. . .

Life Lesson: Next time you are promised a limo, ask questions lots of questions.

Chapter Thirty-One

PRACTICALLY GONE WITH THE WIND

When I was fourteen, my mom got remarried. I was the maid of honor. I resembled Scarlet O'Hara in my hat and off-the-shoulder floor-length lavender dress, made even fuller with a hoop skirt underneath.

The ceremony, although beautiful, was three hours long and mostly in Greek. There was a lot of activity. Cantors were singing, and altar servers kept popping in and out of secret doors with lit candles and incense while the priest rubbed holy oil on anyone within arm's reach.

The next thing I knew, the whole wedding party was holding hands while walking in a circle as the priest chanted something that sounded like, "Sophia". The non-Greek guests looked around, waiting for someone named Sophia to pop out of one of those secret doors, but Sophia was a no-show.

The priest then placed crowns on the bride and groom's heads and may have proclaimed them the prom king and queen. I'm not sure, though, since it was in Greek.

When the ceremony was over, the church emptied quickly. The wedding couple drove off in a shiny white limo. I searched the parking lot for my new brother, who was supposed to give me a ride, but he had taken off without me. I looked for a familiar face but saw none. In a matter of minutes, the parking lot was empty. The wind began gusting, and I had difficulty keeping my giant skirt from blowing over my head. The clouds started rolling in, and it got dark and rainy.

In a panic, I tried to open the doors to the church, but they were locked. I was alone in an unsafe area, on top of a hill, in a storm, with no ride, no phone, or cocktail hour. And I was starving. Apparently, my new brother was also the way he burned rubber out of the parking lot without me.

Then, I saw headlights. I got nervous and hid behind a bush. My impossibly poufy dress stuck out on both sides of the sparse shrubbery giving me away.

It was Father John! I was so happy to see him even though he said something that I had no hope of understanding. It still sounded like he was saying, "Sophia".

I thought, "Can he just let this whole Sophia thing go already? She is not coming." Then I wondered, "Did he think my name was 'Sophia'? Was I supposed to do something during the ceremony?"

At this point, I didn't care what he called me. I just wanted to be warm, dry, and at the reception with everyone else. Thank God he showed up, or I would have been gone with the wind.

Life Lesson: Before you agree to be part of a wedding party, always secure your post-ceremony transportation arrangements.

Chapter Thirty-Two

SLAP A BOW ON IT

We were coming down the home stretch with just one more year left. I had been taking Veronica to classes for religion education for nine years. She had to attend a special mass to complete her requirements for the year. We selected an afternoon mass on the Saturday before Easter, mainly because it was the shortest one. I hoped it would be a light crowd since Easter was the next day, and people would most likely be preparing for the holiday. The year before, we went to a candlelight vigil. It was beautiful, although very crowded, and with so many lit candles inches away from me, I regretted my overzealous spritzing of hairspray, remembering the 'stay away from open flames' warning on the can.

We arrived early and talked quietly, which gave us a chance to get our giggles out of the way. We really should not be allowed to sit next to each other in church. Everything is funnier, with an intensified urge to laugh when you must be quiet.

This mass was to bless the food for Easter Sunday. We watched as parishioners proudly walked into church with wicker baskets ornately decorated with flowers, ribbons, lit candles and placed them on the steps in front of the altar. The baskets contained homemade bread, fruit, dyed hard-boiled eggs, and some had covered dishes. Since the blessing of the food is a Polish tradition, I feared somewhere on the altar was stuffed cabbage. If so, I prayed the lid was on tightly. While delicious, the smell of cabbage can be a little pungent. Not even the incense burning in the church would be able to cover it up.

Veronica and I had been out running errands and came directly to the church. I felt terrible that I didn't bring any food to be blessed. I started laughing as I remembered my turkey in a five-gallon bucket in my garage sitting in a brine. I jokingly asked Veronica if we should go home and get it. She loved the idea and convinced me to do it. We lived close by so we could easily make it back before mass started.

We raced home, and Veronica helped me maneuver the sloshy bucket of turkey into the backseat of my car. Even though it had a lid, she sat next to it to ensure it did not tip over. The last thing I needed was five gallons of raw turkey juice, saturating the interior of my car.

We laughed with anticipation as we drove back to church.

I asked Veronica, "Should we do this?"

"Absolutely!" she responded.

I felt a little self-conscious that my turkey presentation wasn't more elaborate. I am somewhat competitive in the arena of my children's projects. With my expert guidance and creativity, they have won multiple fire prevention poster contests, and they always had the best dioramas, my favorite of which was a 50's ice cream shop scene. I used wafer ice cream cones for stools with Oreos as the seats and red licorice laces to line the countertop. It was impressive.

Remembering that I had bows in the trunk for gift wrapping, I quickly got out of the car. There wasn't much time! I chose a big purple bow and attached it to the lid of the bucket. It was the best I could do and made me feel much more confident.

Together, Veronica and I carried our bucket of turkey into the church through the side door. There was no way I was walking down the center aisle with this. I would have needed a big sip of the sacristy wine first. We discreetly managed to get our bucket onto the altar steps and hurried out the same door we entered. Once outside, we laughed and took a moment to compose ourselves.

Veronica and I decided to enter the church from the main entrance to see our bucket of turkey from a better angle and admire it in all its glory. We would sit in the back of the church in case we had a hard time controlling ourselves.

Biting my bottom lip to keep myself from laughing, we walked through the doors. Touched by the beauty of the scene and the meaning behind the blessing of the food, I smiled as I admired my five-gallon orange bucket from Home Depot with a purple bow amongst the lovely, more traditional baskets. I may not have had the best presentation like I usually do, but I got points for creativity, chutzpah, and poise since I behaved very well during the service.

Life Lesson: Everything looks better with a big bow slapped on it.

Chapter Thirty-Three

FOLLICALLY CHALLENGED

When my first daughter was born, her hair was quite unusual. It was jet black, and her hairline started halfway back on her head. The whole top was short and stood straight up while the sides and back were long. Every time the nurse brought her to me, her hair was wet. The whole nursing staff tried to tame her weird hair, but no one could do anything with it.

The next day, her pediatrician came to see us in the hospital.

He said with a smile, "She looks like an aging rock star!"

I was so insulted. The doctor wasn't wrong, but no new mother wants to hear that.

By the time of Victoria's Christening, the front of her hair filled in so much it looked like she was wearing a hairpiece with a bad comb-over.

My second daughter was also born with a big head of hair; only it made more sense. It was wavy, blonde, and somehow perfectly coiffed when she entered the world.

My mother said, "Her hair looks like Leslie Stahl's from 60 minutes."

By the time Veronica's Christening arrived, her hair had become even more magnificent.

We were lucky enough to have Father Kevin officiate. He was the funniest priest I have ever met. Attending his masses was so hilarious that you felt like you were at a comedy club.

Father Kevin was also follically challenged, but differently from my daughter; he did not have a single hair on his head.

As Father Kevin Christened Veronica while pouring the water over her head, he asked, "Is it wrong to be jealous of a child?"

Whenever he made a joke, he smiled broadly, and his eyes twinkled as he reveled in everyone's laughter.

Father Kevin then unsuccessfully tried to towel dry her giant mop of hair.

"Did anyone bring a hairdryer? Is there a hairstylist in the room? I have no experience in working with hair," he asked.

Life Lesson: My mother says, "It's always about the hair. There's too much in some places and not enough in others."

Chapter Thirty-Four

A MEMORABLE ENTRANCE

The sun was shining through the stained-glass windows lining the church. It was a special day. The children looked precious in their perfectly pressed dark suits and flowing white dresses, ready to receive their First Holy Communion.

Father Frank was in the middle of his sermon. He was proud of the young boys and girls ready to become full members of our faith. As Father spoke with such love and pride for these blessed children, his words filled our hearts with joy.

Suddenly, someone appeared on the altar behind Father Frank. I was confused and wondering what my Aunt Gayle was doing up there? Was she reading from the Gospel? Was she a surprise guest since she attended St. Mary's as a child?

As I tried to make sense of this in my mind, she was briskly escorted from the altar by the communion teacher. I watched the interaction while still trying to understand what was going on.

I could read Aunt Gayle's lips as she said, "Oh my goodness!"

She laughed and waved like a celebrity to the members of the congregation while being directed to sit with our family in the third pew.

When she sat next to me, I asked, "What happened?"

"There were so many entrances from the parking lot. I was running late and rushed through the first set of doors that I saw," she told me.

In her defense, there are three doors from the parking lot that lead directly to the altar. I can understand how it happened. Although, if it were me and I made a grand entrance onto the altar during a service, I would have backed up and hyperventilated in the parking lot for a moment and entered from the back of the church.

Aunt Gayle appearing on the altar in the middle of the service and simply laughing about it was one of the highlights of the communion service, for me at least. She has always been one of my favorite people. Like me, ridiculous things happen to Aunt Gayle, and she just laughs. I learned that from her, and I am so grateful.

Life Lesson: Always make a memorable entrance and if something embarrassing happens, laugh it off.

WHO IS CALLING ME NOW?

Chapter Thirty-Five

STOP ANSWERING THE PHONE!

It was Superbowl Sunday, and we had to hurry to get our bets in for the family football pool.

Scott's father had unfairly accused us of cheating the year before and insisted we fax him our winning team picks and total score before the game started. Scott, the girls, and I wrote our guesses down and were ready to fax it to Pa.

Pa had one of those fax numbers that shared the line with his home phone. I called him and told him that I was sending the fax and not to answer the phone. Simple, right?

I sent the fax, and I heard it ringing in preparation to send the ever-important football pool picks.

Pa picked up the phone with an extraordinarily chipper and drawn out, "Hellllllllo!"

Scott and I could hear his voice over the fax machine. Pa stopped the fax transmission when he answered the phone.

I called Pa back and reminded him not to answer the phone so that the fax could go through.

I resent the fax. The transmission started, and then I heard the chipper 'Helllllo!' He picked up the phone again.

This time, in the background over the fax, I heard Granny's voice.

"Johnny, don't pick up the phone!"

There's that expression; the third time's the charm. I resent it in high hopes it would go through this time.

Again Pa picked and the phone and said, "Hellllllo!"

Scott called his father and told him, "Just let the phone ring. Don't answer it!"

Granny was still yelling in the background, "I keep telling him, but he won't listen."

Now Pa and Granny were arguing. We hoped that would keep Pa busy so the fax could go through.

After a couple more attempts, we had success! Pa was able to refrain from picking up the phone and received our picks for the football pool.

It was far from over. I noticed the fax machine was still attempting to send the fax even though it successfully went through.

I asked Scott, "Should I stop it?"

He smiled and, knowing it would make his father nuts said, "Keep sending the fax."

So, I did, with too much pleasure, admittedly.

We heard the familiar 'Hellllllo.' over the fax machine. We kept sending it, and he kept picking up the phone with his cheerful salutation.

Pa reached his breaking point literally and figuratively. On the last fax attempt, we got one last peppy, 'Helllllo.'

"Jesus, Barb, they are still sending it," he yelled.

Scott, the girls, and I were hysterical. There is something so funny about hearing someone yelling over the fax machine.

Later, Granny called to inform me that I had won the football pool and that they no longer had a fax machine. Pa ripped the fax line out of the wall and threw the fax machine over the deck out of frustration. In all the commotion and destruction, the room needed a fresh coat of paint. Granny thanked me. She wanted to have the room repainted anyway.

Gooooooodbye, fax machine.

Life Lesson: Get a separate line for your fax machine or use fax to email.

Chapter Thirty-Six

NOT WITHOUT MY CRUISE WEAR

It was 6 AM on a Sunday. The phone rang. It wasn't 2 AM, so I knew nothing was wrong. It was more like, "Who the hell is calling me at this hour?"

My mom needed help fast! A limo service picked my parents up at 5 AM. My father and the driver oversaw getting all the luggage into the trunk. Whatever happened, it was my father's fault, according to my mother. She was furious because her suitcase was not in the trunk of the limo when they arrived at the airport.

"Go to my house now! It was dark when we left. The suitcase must be in the driveway. Hurry, the plane is leaving soon," she pleaded with panic in her voice.

Scott and I sprang out of bed, no time for coffee. We had to go!

During the seven-minute ride to my mom's house, I hoped her suitcase was still in the driveway. My parent's house was on top of a steep hill. Her luggage had wheels, and it was windy. I was reminded of when I first started driving, and I kept forgetting to put the emergency brake on, and my car kept rolling out into the street. Luckily, my car hit the curb each time and didn't roll away. But those wheels on suitcases are crazy and turn in all directions. I envisioned her designer suitcase wildly careening to the bottom of the hill. Scott and I simply had no time to search the bushes for my mother's cruise wear.

When we turned the corner, we saw the silhouette of my mom's suitcase all alone in the middle of the driveway. Suddenly, I was annoyed with my father, too. And why didn't the driver see the bag in the headlights as he pulled out of the driveway?

Scott grabbed the suitcase and threw it into the back of his truck. We sped off to the airport, hoping we would make it in time. If my mother had her sequined gown for the captain's dinner, my dad would be off the hook for abandoning her luggage in the dark.

The roads were quiet, and we made it there in record time. When we pulled up in front of the airport drop-off area, a man in uniform rushed over to us. It was the driver. We got a quick "hello" and "thank you very much," and he rushed off with fear in his eyes.

I said a short prayer for him and my dad, "God, please let him make it for everyone's sake."

There were mere minutes left before the plane took off. My mom's suitcase did not make it. Sadly, it was on the next plane.

When my parents boarded the cruise ship, there was still no sign of it. They anxiously waited on the deck watching for the taxi that was supposed to deliver her suitcase. Time was running out. My father offered to share his clothing with my mom, but she was unimpressed and balked at the suggestion that she wear a tuxedo and one of his bathing suits.

The foghorn sounded. Hope faded. But suddenly, a taxi tore up the road and screeched to a halt. A frazzled woman jumped out of the cab and ran towards the ship carrying my mother's abandoned luggage. The foghorn blew again.

"OMG, run faster, the ship is about to leave port," my mother yelled.

The woman made it to the ship and threw the suitcase to a crew member who caught it! My mother's cruise wear made it aboard! Everyone breathed a sigh of relief, especially my dad. The foghorn sounded, and the ship pulled out to sea. It was smooth sailing and sequins the rest of the way. Bon Voyage!

Life Lesson: Always keep particularly close tabs on the whereabouts of your cruise wear, and don't pick up the phone at 6 AM on a Sunday.

Chapter Thirty-Seven

THEY MUST BE DEAD IN A DITCH

We dropped the girls off at Granny and Pa's house for four hours one evening so Scott and I could attend a holiday beefsteak dinner for contractors. The dinner was at the Brownstone, which was only fifteen minutes away from their house.

The food was terrific as always, and the emcee was hilarious. I kept checking my phone to see if Granny had called since it was so loud in the ballroom that I would never hear it ring in my purse.

Before we got up from the table to go home, I checked my phone one more time. There were no phone calls. We thanked the hosts for a fantastic night. I did not notice that Granny called right after I checked my phone and while we were saying goodbye to our friends.

On the short ride back to my in-law's house, Scott and I gossiped and marveled at how delectable the roasted short ribs were.

When we walked through the front door, everyone was crying.

Granny charged over to us and hugged us, saying, "Thank God you are both all right! I didn't know what I was going to do with two small children!"

As Victoria and Veronica fell into our arms sobbing, I asked, "What is going on? Did something happen?"

Granny said, still trying to compose herself, "When you didn't answer your phone, we got worried. Pa and I went over all of the scenarios and concluded that you two drove off the road and were dead in a ditch."

"What?" Scott and I exclaimed at the same time.

"Pa is out searching all of the ditches right now," she said, still distraught.

I wondered where all these deadly ditches were in town? Pa seemed to know, but now he was missing. Did we have to go looking for him now?

Scott and I thanked Granny even though she and Pa terrified the children by telling them we were missing. We decided the next time we planned to go out for the evening we should bring the kids. It would be less traumatizing for everyone.

Life Lesson: Wait longer than fifteen minutes before declaring two adults who have not been out for a while without the kids missing.

THEY'RE ALL ANIMALS

Chapter Thirty-Eight

JUST A WARNING

I opened the front door to see a police officer standing there.

He asked me, "Do you have chickens?"

It was clear that I did; he could see the coop from where he was standing.

"Why are you asking?" I answered, not giving up any information as I lifted my chin and threw back my shoulders.

"There are six hens a few houses down the street. The homeowner called. Are they yours?"

"I doubt it, but I'll check," I said.

I knew darn well the chickens were mine, and so did the officer, but I was playing it cool for some reason. When I feel threatened in any way, my Jersey girl attitude kicks in whether I am wearing my big hoop earrings or not. It's on autopilot.

I went to the coop and did a headcount. Dammit, the escaped hens were mine.

"I think they're mine," I told the officer as I started to thaw slowly but kept my guard up just in case there was trouble.

I grabbed a box of cheerios to shake and entice the chickens to follow me home. They are very snack-driven, so I thought it would be easy. As I got closer to my neighbor's house, I recognized my girls. They were digging for worms, pecking the ground with their fluffy butts pointing up. They were onto something so delicious that they completely ignored me as I shook the box of cereal. My neighbor, the officer, and I tried to catch them, but they kept averting us. They were misbehaving.

I joked with the officer, "It might just be easier to shoot them."

The officer managed to catch one of the chickens and put her in the back of his car.

"That's going to be messy," I told him.

"That's OK," he said, "I'm not cleaning it."

I laughed but hoped he didn't think I was going to clean it.

I noticed that it was 2:55 PM, and I had to pick up my girls from school. The officer had only caught three hens, and the other three were still evading arrest.

I apologized, "I have to leave now to pick up my daughters." I handed him the box of cheerios just in case he needed them.

When I got home from school, I saw the cheerios on my patio table, and all six hens were back in the coop with their friends. They must have gotten off with just a warning, this time.

Life Lesson: Play it cool; admit to nothing.

Chapter Thirty-Nine

I'M A STAR, DAMMIT

"You want to use our goat in your school play?" I asked with disbelief. "She's not house trained. She'll make a mess," I said.

The theater director at our local high school was unphased. "It's not a problem. We will clean up after her," he assured me. "All you have to do is bring the white goat to school for rehearsal three times and then to the four live shows."

Still unsure, I told him that our white goat, Lady Godiva, was quite stubborn. If she didn't want to do something, she would lock her legs and become immovable while screaming until she got her way.

"Can't you just use a stuffed goat?" I asked. "It seems like it would be so much easier all around."

No, he wanted a live goat and needed Lady Godiva in his school production. I told him that our other goat, Sassy, would be a better choice. She wasn't white; she was black and grey but would be easier to work with than her temperamental sidekick, Lady Godiva.

"Fine, we will be happy to work with Sassy," he said.

On the night of Sassy's first rehearsal, Scott got home from work, showered, ate, and was ready at 6 PM to bring the unexpected star to meet the cast. I buckled up the then three-year-old Victoria while Scott walked Sassy on a leash to the driveway. I was not wild about having a goat in my new vehicle, but it was a short drive, thankfully. Scott got into the back of my SUV first, and I helped Sassy onto his lap. She seemed concerned, unsure of where we were going.

When we arrived at the high school, we were greeted by the very excited students and led to a classroom which would be Sassy's dressing room. She could relax and wait for her big scene. Sassy was getting the star treatment and loved all the attention, as was little Victoria. The kids made a big fuss over her, as well.

It was time for Sassy to practice her scene. She was tentative as she entered the backstage area and waited for her cue. Sassy did not have any lines but improvised with perfectly timed bleats as she walked across the stage while the spotlight followed her. Sassy was a natural! The cast cheered and gathered around her. Sassy was so proud of herself. She wasn't sure what she did, but apparently, it was spectacular, and she was rewarded with some salty crackers.

For the following two days, at 6 PM, we brought Sassy to rehearsal. She was more at ease each time and seemed to enjoy the attention and showing off her acting chops. She was a star, and everyone agreed.

At last, opening night arrived. Scott and I were nervous, hoping that Sassy played her part as expected. Sassy, on the other hand, was not scared; she was a professional, after all.

We walked her to the backstage area, left her with her castmates, and hugged her while wishing her good luck. Scott, Victoria, and I went to sit with the audience and anxiously awaited Sassy's big debut. When she first stepped on stage, she froze.

"Oh no!" I said.

But, with an encouraging tug of her leash, she got into character and walked across the stage with such poise and grace letting out one loud bleat as the audience laughed and cheered for her. A star was born! We were so proud of our girl.

Sassy took her acting role very seriously. She also learned to tell time because she waited at the gate at 6 PM for us to drive her to her final performances.

On the day after her final curtain call, Sassy was waiting at the gate at 6 PM. She became visibly upset and cried as if telling us, "The show can't go on without me! I am a star, dammit!"

For the next week, we went out at 6 PM and played with Sassy, so she knew that she was still a star on stage and off.

Life Lesson: Don't be a drama queen.

Chapter Forty

TONE DOWN THE SPARKLES

I'll never learn. Scott constantly reprimands me for always wearing the wrong footwear. I enjoy wearing high heel boots, platforms, and flip-flops, even when collecting eggs in the chicken coop.

I had just picked the girls up from school, and they went into the house for a snack. I heard the chickens making a fuss, so I went up to the coop to see what the problem was and collect the eggs. I opened the lock on the coop door, but I forgot to pull the latch forward to prevent the door from slamming shut and locking me inside the coop.

The door slammed behind me.

"Oh no! I'm locked in," I yelled.

I was instantly annoyed with Scott for this predicament since he developed this weird locking system on the coop door to keep the bears out. The only problem was it was easy to get trapped inside like I was now.

I called out to the girls through the coop window. No humans came to my rescue; however, all the chickens ran into the coop, not to help me, just hoping I had a treat for them. I didn't have any treats, but the chickens started coming closer and closer. They were attracted to my red shiny painted toenails and wedge flip flops bedazzled with sparkly crystals.

"Help!" I screamed as twenty-five chickens were surrounding me.

Still, no one came. One of the chickens jumped up and pecked me in the butt. Dammit, I also had rhinestones on the back pockets of my jeans.

The chickens were closing in, obsessed with my overly sparkly flip flops and back pockets. They took turns trying to peck at my feet as I jumped up and down, waving my arms and screaming.

I tried to push out the chicken wire in the window but struggled. Scott used so many heavy-duty staples, creating quite a fortress designed to keep chicken-loving wild animals out, but it made it difficult to escape.

With the chickens continuing to close in, I picked up a shovel to push them away from me.

"Stay back," I yelled.

I had to think of something fast. Luckily, I could see one of the staples coming loose and kept pushing on the metal wire as hard as I could. In between fighting off the chickens and creating an escape plan, I made an opening wide enough to slip through. Only the window was too high. I looked around for something to stand on as the chickens tried pecking at my shoes.

The only thing I could find was their water bucket. I dumped the water and flipped it upside down to stand on it. It was just tall enough for me to reach the window and climb out to safety.

When I went into the house, the girls were watching TV and eating cereal.

"I was locked in the coop. Didn't you hear me screaming?" I asked.

"I thought I heard something," Victoria said unconcerned, focusing on *Kim Possible*.

"OMG, I could have been pecked to death because of my sparkly shoes," I replied.

"Daddy told you not to wear flip-flops in the coop," Veronica reminded me. She was right.

"That doesn't mean I should be attacked by chickens, though," I replied.

When Scott got home, he changed the lock on the coop, knowing full well that even after being tormented by the sparkle-crazed chickens, I would still wear the most inappropriate footwear in most situations, especially in the chicken coop.

Life Lesson: Tone down the sparkles just a bit for your own safety and always have a good exit plan.

Chapter Forty-One

LITTLE LIARS

Our rabbit, Buns, was so sweet. Not that I ever heard of a vicious rabbit, but Buns was extraordinary. Scott would let him out of his cage to run around the yard, and Buns would put himself back in his coop when he was tired.

I loved watching him from inside the house. He had a good time mingling with the outdoor creatures but looked totally out of place with his white fur and pink eyes. Every time I looked out the window, he was up to something new. Sometimes, he would go into the pen and nap under the dogwood tree with our two goats. I often rescued him when Sassy, the goat, would pick him up by his ears and walk around with him. Sometimes, he would go into the chicken coup and see if the hens had any good snacks like fresh fruit or veggies. Ripe bananas and pears were his favorite treat. Buns chased squirrels, hung out with wild turkeys, and touched noses with the deer. He was always so happy bouncing around in the grass while enjoying the fresh air and warm sun on his back.

When Buns was thirteen years old, he began slowing down. We wanted to mate him so a part of him would continue, although no rabbit would ever be as unique as Buns.

I called a local farm that had rabbits for sale, and a lovely woman answered the phone.

"Do you have any white rabbits?" I inquired.

The woman said, "We have plenty of rabbits."

I repeated, "Are they white?"

The woman told me, "I do not think that the color makes any difference."

"My husband wants a white rabbit," I told her again.

"I do not think that the color makes any difference," she repeated.

"I want to pick a rabbit out myself," I told her.

I could tell she was annoyed by my insistence that the rabbit was white and hand-selected by me.

"If you want to pick up a rabbit today, you have to pick from the rabbits that are all ready to go," she said impatiently.

I was confused for a moment, wondering what 'all ready to go' meant. Were the bunny's suitcases already packed?

This whole conversation was odd. Then I realized what was happening. I was talking about a pet rabbit, and the woman was referring to a butchered rabbit since they also had a farm store.

I clarified, "I want my rabbit alive and not in waxed paper for dinner."

Laughing, she said, "Come down anytime."

When I arrived at the farm, Jimmy, the head honcho of the rabbits, had left for lunch. I was brought to a pen by another man and told to select whichever female rabbit I wanted. There were no white bunnies, but a grey one caught my eye. I could not decide if she was funny-looking or the most stunning rabbit I had ever seen. Her coat was so luxurious, with the tips of her fur seemingly frosted. She had impossibly high cheekbones, a pointy head, and giant ears. Her body was long and lean. Her eyelashes were jet black, very full, and so long that she looked like she was wearing false eyelashes.

I said, "I'll take that one," pointing to the unusual-looking rabbit.

The man put her in a box, not in waxed paper like the woman on the phone was planning, and I headed home.

The next day, we introduced old man Buns to the young supermodel rabbit we named April. He had no idea what to do with such a hottie. Scott and I waited for nature to take its course. Nothing happened.

Finally, there was action. But Buns was doing it all wrong. Perhaps it was because Buns was older? Maybe it was because he was blind in one eye and couldn't see what he was doing? Maybe it was because he had no experience and was nervous? He was humping April's head, and she was unimpressed. I tried to position them correctly in what suddenly felt like a ménage à trois. I was willing to do my part, but still, Buns couldn't make it happen.

I called Jimmy and arranged to bring April down for a rendezvous with a young stud who could get the job done.

When I arrived, and Jimmy opened the box, he gasped, "You're the one who took my prized rabbit."

He was heartbroken but let me keep her anyway since it was his fault for putting April into the cage with the ordinary rabbits.

Scott and I waited for the baby bunnies to arrive. In the meantime, he constructed a nesting box with a top for privacy and warmth and filled it with hay. We kept watching April for signs that the babies were coming. We never saw her go into the nesting box. She was not missing any fur from making a nest for the babies. The time had well passed when April should have given birth, and still, we did not see any babies.

One day, I heard scratching in the nesting box.

"Scott, I think there is a mouse in the nesting box."

Scott heard the scratching and said, "Yes, that's a mouse!"

He picked up the nesting box and walked into the freshly tilled garden.

I watched as he turned the box upside down and repeatedly shook it as hard as he could while yelling, "Get out, you little bastard!"

Hay, fur, and tiny grey mouse-sized creatures flew out of the box into the soft soil. There were five tiny baby bunnies about two inches long. The poor little things were horrified, as were we.

The second they hit the ground; they took off in all different directions. Wow, those babies could run fast! The first one was easy to catch since it fell into a footprint in the fresh soil and could not get out. Two ran into the sticker bushes, and the other two ran straight into the woods. Somehow, we caught the impossibly petite petrified bunnies.

Scott reassembled the nesting box that he had abruptly shaken apart and tucked the bunnies back into their nest safe and sound. He apologized to April for the rude awakening her babies experienced on their first outing.

Scott may have unconventional rabbit rearing techniques, but he is still the best rabbit whisperer in Northern New Jersey. Ask anyone, just not the bunnies. They're little liars.

Life Lesson: Try using some darn common sense.

PERFECTLY TERRIBLE TIMING

Chapter Forty-Two

GUILTY UNTIL PROVEN INNOCENT

My father had recently passed away, and I thought it would be nice to go out to eat with my mom and spend time together. We decided to go to the buffet at the Grand Chalet, which always offered a delicious array of cuisines.

We returned to our table with our plates piled high with delectable meats, crisp salads, al dente pasta, fresh vegetables, and just-baked bread.

It was incredibly crowded, and the restaurant was bustling with the happy sounds of people talking and dishes clanking as everyone enjoyed their meals.

Sitting across from my mother, I watched in absolute shock as she rocked back and forth from side to side three times. Each time she rocked, she passed gas very loudly. It was like a foghorn. I was further appalled when she showed no remorse and started to dig into her food. I thought she had been spending too much time alone and forgot her manners which seemed odd since my mother is usually so elegant.

Then I heard the laughter from different parts of the room. I could feel my face get hot, my eyes widened, and my mouth hung open.

I slowly glanced to the right, the look of horror still on my face, and then I heard the sound again.

The man at the table next to us was blowing his nose so loudly. Moments before, my mother just happened to move in unison with his nose-blowing, making her look guilty of farting with wild abandon in public.

His eyes met mine. He saw the look on my face and became embarrassed, thinking I was so disgusted by his nose blowing at the table.

I rejoiced inside because this meant that my mother was still elegant.

I wanted so desperately to tell her what happened, but the obnoxious nose blower was glaring at me, thinking I was talking about him. When he finally left, I was able to share the story with my mother. We laughed, but my mother begged me not to repeat the story because she felt that her guilt would still be inferred although she was innocent. She was just pulling her chair in as she rocked back and forth, after all, not letting one rip.

Truthfully, we would have gotten into a fight about this. I know what I heard and what I saw, but it was just the unfortunate timing that made her look guilty as hell. Thank goodness I saw the truth that my mother was innocent, and her wrongfully tarnished reputation was quickly restored. Such a relief!

Life Lesson: Don't believe what you see and hear; only believe what you smell.

Chapter Forty-Three

WOOZY

I did not invite Scott to come to the hospital with me for our second daughter's birth. I told him I would call when it was time. I knew it would be easier that way after his lackluster performance when our first daughter was born.

Scott starts to feel unwell the second he steps into a hospital, making him useless. He had two jobs during the birth; to give me oxygen and to support my right knee. He tried, but Scott became woozy in less than one minute, and the nurses escorted him to a recliner. They also gave him a pillow, blanket, juice, and a cookie.

I was getting annoyed that the spotlight was still on Scott as the nurses continued to fuss over him. Meanwhile, I was about to pop out a tiny human.

"He is a little dizzy. He will be fine," I yelled as another contraction came.

We all decided that it would be best for everyone if Scott just slept. It was 3 AM, and he worked all day, plus it was clear that he was not going to be any help whatsoever.

I ended up giving myself oxygen and holding my knee myself. We woke Scott right before Victoria was born.

When it was time to go to the hospital to have Veronica, Scott stayed home and watched Victoria, and my mom came to the hospital with me.

Around 5:30 AM, my mom called Scott and told him it was time. Our house was only ten minutes away, so he had time to arrive before Veronica's birth.

When he was on his way to the hospital, Veronica was born. My mom called to tell him. About twenty minutes later, Scott showed up with a cup of coffee in his hand, and Victoria was eating a doughnut.

"Are you serious? You stopped for coffee first and missed the birth? And why is Victoria still wearing her clothes from yesterday?" I asked.

Scott said, "You have no idea what I have been through with Victoria. She refused to take her shirt off because it was her favorite, so I just let her sleep in it. Right before we were about to leave this morning, Victoria had a tantrum and insisted that I find her eagle hat. I couldn't understand what she was saying since I had never seen it before. I frantically searched the whole house and finally found it in your car. Halfway here, your mother called and said Veronica had arrived. At that point, I just stopped for coffee. I desperately needed it."

"She doesn't care about that hat at all. That's why it was in my trunk," I told Scott.

It was clear that Victoria was not thrilled about her new sister and was not rushing to meet her.

When I introduced Victoria to her, she said, "What's that?" She warmed up to Veronica slightly and said, "Fine, we can keep her, but you can't hold her much, and she has to live with the goats in the barn."

I laughed to myself, thinking that this was like the *Seinfeld* episode when Elaine's boyfriend was rushed to the hospital for emergency surgery, and she stopped for Jujubes before going to see him. On the show, he was so mad, but I was too woozy to be annoyed.

Besides, I now had to figure out who would be the better roommate for Veronica, her sister, or the goats. So far, it was looking like the goats.

Life Lesson: If you must rush to the hospital to see someone but stop for a snack first, finish it before going in.

Chapter Forty-Four

BODY BAGS

My daughter Veronica was watching *Hawaii 5-0* in the family room. In this episode, a serial killer left the remains of his victims in enormous black garbage bags on the side of the road.

When Veronica finished watching TV, she went up to her room even though she was still a little scared from the show. I heard her open her bedroom door and scream.

I called upstairs to make sure she was OK.

"OMG! Why is this in my room?" she yelled with fear in her voice.

I was expecting an insect. Veronica hates bugs and needs someone brave to remove them and return them to their natural habitat. She won't let us kill them.

I quickly ran up the stairs to see what had frightened her. She pointed to the two industrial black garbage bags that were not there when she left her room earlier.

"What's in those bags?" I asked.

Veronica had no idea and was too afraid to open them. She described the show she had just watched. I understood her discomfort, and I didn't want to open them either.

Hearing the commotion, Scott walked into her room and solved the mystery.

"I was up in the attic and brought down the outdoor Christmas lights. I just put them in Veronica's room until I could take them downstairs later. They are too big to leave in the hallway," he said.

Veronica was relieved that the big black trash bags that mysteriously showed up in her room were just innocuous holiday decorations, not victims of a crazed killer. Although unfortunate, it was terribly perfect timing, and we all had a good laugh.

Life Lesson: If you leave suspiciously stuffed industrial black garbage bags that are big enough to fit dismembered bodies in someone's bedroom, warn them first. It's the right thing to do.

Chapter Forty-Five

WAIT, BEFORE YOU GO...

My grandmother was known for her sausage stuffing. She only made it on Thanksgiving. We had a big family, and everyone waited all year long for her perfectly moist seasoned turkey stuffing with chunks of sweet and hot sausage. We would have been happy if that was all she served for the holidays; it was that extraordinary!

Unfortunately, every Thanksgiving, a couple and their two grown children came for dinner. They were all seemingly seven feet tall. Every year, they devoured the stuffing but were polite enough to leave a couple of tablespoons for each of us. It was a tease. We began to resent them. We urged Grandma to stop inviting these ravenous giants or at least make more stuffing. She refused on both counts.

My grandmother planned to take this recipe to her grave. She never made it in front of anyone. It was the only recipe anyone ever asked her for, and she was not divulging her stuffing recipe, not even to her children and grandchildren.

Later in her life, Grandma developed emphysema and had to be on oxygen. She suffered from congestive heart failure and other issues, as well. When Grandma's time on this earth was coming to an end, we all sat by her bedside and played her favorite games; Upwords and Rummy

500. We laughed as we talked about funny memories and got the chance to tell her how much we loved her.

The time came, and it was awkward, but my aunt asked, “Wait, before you go, can we have your stuffing recipe?”

“No,” she replied without remorse.

We threatened to put a kink in her oxygen line if she did not comply. We gave her time to think about it but were ready to do whatever it took to obtain her secret recipe.

Luckily, just before she left to be with Jesus, she came to her senses. Her last words were her instructions on making her secret recipe. My aunt carefully wrote it down.

Even though she gave us the recipe, Grandma’s stuffing was still the best. I suspect she left out a special ingredient either on purpose or due to the temporary lack of oxygen.

Her title as “The Supreme Sausage Stuffing Queen” is forever safe. The rest of the family even, with the recipe, are merely runners up.

Life Lesson: Don’t trust your grandma when she shares a recipe. She may leave an important ingredient out so that everyone remembers her version as the very best.

Chapter Forty-Six

IT DOESN'T MAKE SENSE

"I don't understand; it doesn't make sense," she said to her husband, walking out of the store.

She was confused, and I could sense fearing for her sanity. I completely understood because the same thing that happened to her had just happened to me.

Scott, the girls, and I were on our way back from Lancaster, PA, and we stopped at a smokehouse to get fresh chicken, smoked pork chops, and skirt steak. A pleasant man with red hair, glasses, and a light blue plain t-shirt took my order and wrapped it nicely for me. He asked me to meet him at the register on the other side of the store. On the way, I passed Scott as he was gently squeezing a molasses crinkle cookie to see if it was the right combination of tender and chewy.

I saw Victoria and Veronica looking at a rack of upsetting things pickled in jars. I couldn't imagine anything on that rack to be a big seller.

The ginger-haired man rang up my order, and I paid him. He said "goodbye," turned around and walked through the door into the back-room. He was gone.

I went to see what the girls were laughing at, pickled sheep's eyeballs, I assumed. I walked over to them.

"Look at this!" Victoria said, holding up a jar of pickled eyeballs.

Yes, I was right. I know my girls.

We were laughing, trying to decide what we would eat from the rack of unusual jarred items if forced.

Then I saw him. But it couldn't be. It's impossible. The red-haired man with the glasses and the plain light blue t-shirt was sitting at his desk. How did he do that? He walked the other way and left the store. He didn't pass me. I would have seen him.

The girls were talking to me, but I couldn't hear what they were saying. I was going over everything in my head. I knew I saw him leave. OMG, am I losing my mind? Did I black out momentarily from the scary pickled things in the jars?

I went to find Scott to talk this through with him. I saw him in the honey aisle.

"You have to come with me," I said to him.

As we walked, I told him what had happened, and as we came around the corner, it all made sense.

There were two of them, identical and I mean identical twins, right down to the plain light blue t-shirt. The twin who left had come back and was talking to his twin at the desk.

I was very relieved that I caught them together, so I knew I wasn't crazy. But suddenly, I felt a little angry. That was sort of mean. Did the adult twins have to wear the same outfit? It was not a uniform; everyone else had their own unique style. Did they do this on purpose? Does mommy still buy her middle-aged boys matching clothes?

We headed towards the door laughing when I overheard the confused woman talking to her husband.

"They're twins; you're fine," I said.

The woman laughed and let out a sigh of relief, just like I had moments earlier.

Life Lesson: You're not crazy. There is a reasonable explanation.

I WIN, YOU LOSE

Chapter Forty-Seven

DAMN, I'M GOOD

I saw a white wrought iron set with a couch, two chairs, and a table on Facebook Marketplace. It was just what I was looking for to put on my front porch. I contacted the owner and arranged for Scott to pick up the set on the way home from work later that day.

When Scott arrived to pick up the set, he called me and asked, "Are you sure you want this?"

"Yes, I saw several pictures on Facebook. I want it," I confirmed.

"OK," he said with doubt in his voice.

I should have asked more questions, but I just hung up the phone.

When Scott pulled into the driveway, I sprinted outside in excitement to see my new set.

As he was getting out of his truck, I asked, "Where is it?"

"It's in the back of the truck," he answered.

Perplexed, I watched as he opened the tailgate and began pulling out a small couch, two tiny chairs, and a little table.

"What the hell is that?" I asked.

"It's the couch set you asked me to pick up," he answered.

"It can't be!" I said in shock, looking at the wrought iron set that was only slightly larger than a child's playset. The back of the couch and chairs came up to the middle of Scott's thigh.

"Why do you think I called you to confirm that you wanted this ridiculous thing?" he asked.

"You never mentioned it was so tiny. It looked like it was normal sized in the picture," I said, pulling out my phone to show Scott the listing.

Dammit, I was fooled again by the magic of photography. The previous owner of this silly set was clearly a real estate photographer and gifted at making things look so large and roomy.

It was my turn now to take very deceiving photographs of this stupid set I bought. I got my angles just right by taking the pictures from below to create the illusion that it was a standard size and would be comfortable for an adult. I posted the listing, pricing it $25 less than what I paid.

I got a bite after just ten minutes. A woman wanted to put it on her small balcony and asked if I thought it would fit.

"Oh, it will fit," I assured her. I laughed to myself, thinking, "The real question is are you going to fit in it, lady?"

The woman said she would come right over. I went outside to position the set properly so it would look as large as possible. I moved the big pots of plants on my porch and replaced them with small pots hoping to create the illusion that the set was much larger than it was.

When the woman arrived, I led her to the front porch as we made small talk. We were both laughing and smiling. I did my best to build rapport on the short walk from the driveway to the porch. I watched her expression change when she saw the set. I couldn't help but notice that she was a full-figured woman, looking even more so standing next to the petite couch.

To interrupt her train of thought, I kept talking. “Isn't it pretty?

She nodded hesitantly.

“The cushions are brand new and so cheerful with the bright colored flowers,” I continued.

She agreed with another nod.

“It’s just the right size for your small balcony, just like I told you,” I went on.

“Yes, it will fit,” she replied, warming up slightly to the idea.

“Let me help you get it into your car,” I said enthusiastically. I held my breath waiting for her reply.

“OK,” she said, still not 100% convinced as she picked up both chairs and headed to her car.

I moved with the speed of an Olympic marathon runner as I loaded the couch and table into her car. Still unsure, she handed me the money and drove off.

I happily waved, thinking, “Damn, I’m good.”

Life Lesson: Never believe what you see in pictures.

Chapter Forty-Eight

NOW THAT'S COMPETITIVE

"You have to watch this new show, *Squid Games*," my daughter Veronica exclaimed. "You would love it," she continued.

"What's it about?" I asked.

"People who are heavily in debt compete against each other in children's games, like leapfrog and red light, green light. The winner gets all their debt paid off, and the losers are instantly killed. Sometimes they are shot, or the floor opens, and they fall to their death. It just depends on the game."

"Why do you think I would love this show?" I asked.

"You are so competitive, especially in cards. You never let Victoria and I win games when we were little," she replied.

"That is untrue. I let you both win until you were old enough to handle crushing defeat, around eight years old," I reminded Veronica. While I enjoy winning, having my opponent killed if they lost would not give me pleasure. I would be satisfied just knowing that I won. After all, you and your sister are still alive," I teased.

"This show is animated, right?" I confirmed.

"No, it's real. That's what makes it so good," Veronica said.

"What! How is this allowed to be a show? Who are you?" I exclaimed.

I was horrified that my Veronica, who is usually so compassionate, caring, and sensitive, was not bothered by watching people killed for losing a game.

Veronica laughed, "The people are real. The show is not."

Relieved, I said, "Thank God!" "Do you want to play cards?" I asked. "I promise I won't shoot," I joked.

Veronica declined. She can be a sore loser at times.

Life Lesson: A little competition is good, but fighting to the death is overkill, literally.

Chapter Forty-Nine

BETTER LUCK NEXT TIME, BUDDY

After Christmas, Scott, our two girls, and I went to Cabela's in Pennsylvania to use the gift cards he received. He always needs more fishing gear and new work boots.

The tempting aroma of hot candied nuts and fresh sweet kettle corn welcomed us upon entering Cabela's. Once upstairs, the scent of homemade fudge filled the air. As we neared the upstairs restaurant, the sweet aroma of the fudge mingled with the pungent smell of the sauerkraut and pork buffet, which was, unfortunately, the special of the day. Not surprisingly, we were no longer hungry.

The girls and Scott walked towards the shooting range for target practice, and I wandered into the camping section. They had a massive collection of cast iron skillets, pans, and Dutch ovens.

It reminded me of Sunday mornings at my grandparent's house. My grandfather always made the fluffiest pancakes with crisp edges in his electric cast iron skillet, which was over two feet in diameter. The pancakes, salty bacon, and strong coffee were the best smell to awaken to in the morning. The whole family would gather around the kitchen table and enjoy lively conversation, laughter, and the warmth from the wood-burning stove.

My girls interrupted my trip down memory lane when they came over to show me a funny mug that said, “Sorry about the things I said when we were folding up the tent.” It was amusing since I am always Scott’s assistant for projects, so I completely understand that.

After shopping, we were hungry despite the odd combination of fudge, sauerkraut, and pork still lingering in the air. We opted for iced tea, deep-fried cornmeal-crusted pickles, and burgers at the Red Robin next door.

As we were leaving the restaurant, Scott saw a Walmart, and we all went in to help him get motor oil for his truck. The girls went with him to the dull automotive aisle while I ventured off to look for new towels.

In the towel aisle, there was a mother and her son. I guessed his age to be around nineteen or so. As I decided whether to get grey towels instead of the burgundy color I usually get, I heard the teen chuckle. I looked up to see him reach towards a dancing cactus. It was a foot tall and made of bright green felt with outstretched cactus arms. It had a red scarf, a Santa hat, and giant surprised eyes. When the young man squeezed the Christmas cactus’s hand, it played *Feliz Navidad*. The cactus had impressive moves. It shimmied as it waved its arms and shook its hips to the beat. The boy laughed as he mimicked the dance moves, although he could not get into the groove quite like the cactus. I was mesmerized by the dancing cactus and desperately wanted to have it. It was after the holidays, and I was sure it was the only one left in the store.

I watched closely as his mother called him to the end of the aisle to look at a shower curtain. I knew it was time to make my move. I casually pushed my cart next to the dancing cactus and pretended to look at a hideous rug. With the boy’s back turned, I reached for the cactus and triumphantly put it into my cart. I turned around and exited at the other end of the aisle to avoid the mother and son duo.

I quickened my pace and raced to the automotive aisle with my new treasure. Scott and the girls were still there. I pressed the button on its hand, and the cactus happily swayed its hips as the cheerful Christmas song played. We all laughed, danced, and agreed the festive cactus was coming home with us. Still laughing and dancing to the music, we exited the automotive aisle.

To my shock, the young man was coming towards us. He looked longingly at the cactus as it wildly danced in my cart, then looked right at me, his eyes slanted with displeasure.

My eyes got as big as the eyes on the cactus, and I froze for a second. I quickly composed myself and remembered who I was. I am a Jersey girl, dammit. This Pennsylvania boy was no match for me. Although I was not wearing my giant hoops, red lipstick, and high heels, I knew I still had the upper hand. I stood tall, lifted my chin, and challenged him with my best tough girl, *Oh yeah, and what are YOU going to do about it?* look.

Of course, I was extra brave because my 6' 4" husband was right behind me. No one was getting that cactus away from me. NO ONE! He sensed it was fruitless. Between the giant man and the wild-eyed redhead, he knew he didn't have what it took to wrestle the most fabulous dancing cactus ever away from us. He wisely backed off.

Better luck next time, buddy. You are no match for a Jersey girl with the last dancing cactus in Walmart securely in her cart. Sorry, not sorry.

Life Lesson: Jersey girls always win.

ABOUT THE AUTHOR

Kimberly Vuz is the owner of Inside Out Hypnosis, LLC. She is certified as a Consulting Hypnotist, Emotional Freedom Technique Practitioner, Health Coach, and Life Coach. She also has a B.A. in Communication.

As a former 'push her feelings down and never ask for help' kind of girl, Kimberly knows personally how tremendous stress, fear, and unresolved past hurts make it challenging to focus, function at your highest level, and find the right answers within you to create a life of joy and success.

She helps overwhelmed women identify and resolve the root causes behind their destructive behaviors and fears so they can make positive, lasting changes enabling them to consistently crush their goals. She has also recently begun offering stress management programs to companies to increase their employees' happiness, productivity, and communication.

One of Kimberly's greatest gifts is helping her clients find humor in life while extracting valuable lessons and deep insights so they can unlock their inner power. Her private sessions are light-hearted as she helps clients work through serious issues while providing a safe, friendly atmosphere.

Kimberly lives in Northern New Jersey with her husband, two teenage daughters, a flock of chickens, and four high-maintenance cats. She loves to mountain bike, cook and has recently taken up an interest in photography. Of course, her favorite thing is game night with her hilarious family.

To book a complimentary Discovery Call, visit: www.insideouthypnosis.com

To purchase fun *You're Pretty But Dumb* gifts and gear visit: www.prettybutdumb.com

Made in USA - Kendallville, IN
37228_9781737111733
12.20.2021 2050